making **metal** jewelry

how to stamp, fold, forge and form metal jewelry designs

jen cushman

NORTH LIGHT BOOKS

Cincinnati, Ohio

contents

the thrill of metal—my story

My first encounter with metalsmithing was in 2005 at a national art retreat with mixed-media artist and metalsmith Susan Lenart Kazmer. I had been making jewelry as a hobby since I was a teenager, so when Susan's description listed it as an intermediate-level class, I was sure I had the skills. Holy cow . . . was I mistaken. During class I felt akin to Dorothy when she cried, "Toto, I don't think we're in Kansas any longer!"

I struggled that day with my basic skills, but there was also something magical that happened. Students were lined up with fistfuls of wire in hand, patiently waiting their turns at the torches to draw a bead on the ends of their wire. The moment I dipped into that blue flame and watched the wire ball up and roll in on itself, was, literally, the minute my creative life changed. I felt like a bolt of lightning hit me between the eyes and all I wanted was to learn more. (I was fortunate to join Susan in 2009 as a business partner, and she continues to inspire me with her innovative techniques.)

After that art-retreat class, I bought a plumber's torch, sheet metal and wire from the hardware store and went home to practice my new skills. I scoured bookstores for a beginning metalsmithing book, but all I found were books overly detailed for my beginning needs.

I registered for a silversmithing class at my local community college. My instructor was a third-generation goldsmith, and I never once doubted his educational and professional credentials. As I've learned to work metal, his precision and perfectionism still boggle my mind.

On my first day of class, I was instructed to make a bezel-set ring. I struggled with the jeweler's saw, snapping one thin blade after another. I was so frustrated during my third class that I must have let out a long, loud sigh, and my professor inquired as to what was wrong. At my wit's end, I said, "This just isn't any *fun*." He looked me squarely in the eye and dryly replied, "Making jewelry is not fun."

I was stunned into silence. I packed my tools and left my college class that day wondering if I should give up and return to my first loves of mixed-media paper crafting and collage.

Sheer tenacity kept me from quitting, however and I finished up the semester making three ugly bezel-set rings with semiprecious stones and a fairly decent bracelet.

With these experiences, I bet you're wondering why I would ever wish to write a book on making metal jewelry. The reason is simple: Manipulating metal stirs my soul with a sense of wonder and awe. Shaping, forming, annealing, forging and folding a solid piece of metal is not only fun, it's downright thrilling!

I have one simple goal for this book: I want metalworking to bring you the same joy that it brings me. I'm not a master metalsmith or studio jeweler by any means. While I have definitely learned the "right way," meaning the safe way, to do certain techniques—such as working with fire or using chemicals, and I will keep safety in mind throughout this book—this book is written for other creative people, like myself, who want to explore metal's potential and do so in *their own* way.

metal fundamentals

When I first started learning about metalworking, I wanted to jump right in and build complicated pieces that were a little over my head for my skills at the time. It's just the type of artist I am—always wanting to go from 0 to 100 in under 60 seconds. It's my hope that the information in this book will save you not only time, but the costly mistakes that I learned the hard way. Before we jump right into the projects—which I know you really, really want to do—let's first spend some time reviewing metalworking fundamentals. In this section, you'll learn about types and gauges of metals, necessary tools for metalworking and basic techniques that you'll turn to time and again for making metal jewelry.

types of metal

When first learning about metalsmithing, it's helpful to look at a piece of jewelry you admire and study the individual components of the piece. Even the most detailed and layered work can be analyzed and broken down to jewelry basics when you know what they are.

At its most fundamental, metal jewelry begins with either metal sheet or wire. As you go through this book, you will see these are the starting points for all twenty-two projects. Take note, as this simple principle will help tremendously as you continue to learn new techniques to manipulate metal and build beautiful jewelry.

Sterling silver, which is an alloy (or mixture) of silver and copper, is the metal most jewelers prefer to work with because not only is it a gorgeous-looking white metal, but it's smooth and malleable. The price of metals, and in particular sterling silver, has risen tremendously in the past few years, which means many artists are again turning to base metals: copper, brass, aluminum and nickel silver. In addition to sterling silver, my other favorite metal to use is bronze, which is an alloy of copper and tin. Not only is it inexpensive compared to sterling silver, it patinas beautifully and wears well. I adore the contrasting look of mixed metals, which is why you will see all of these metals used. Also, because of the way the projects are done, feel free to switch up the metal in the designs. Just because my projects' instructions calls for bronze or sterling silver doesn't mean you have to use it, too.

Metal sheet and wire are sold in gauges, with the most common unit of measure being the Brown and Sharpe (aka, the B&S) gauge. When ordering from jewelry-supply stores, you'll need to be familiar with this system because it's how you'll buy your metals. The higher the B&S number, the thinner the gauge; therefore, a wire gauge of 8 is a much heavier, thicker piece of metal than a 22-gauge.

Wire comes in a variety of styles, from round, square, oval, triangular, flat and half-round and also comes in dead soft, half-hard and hard. When I order wire from a jewelry supply store, I usually order like this: 3' (0.9m) of sterling silver, round, 20-gauge, dead soft. I also buy prepackaged spools of bronze wire and keep gauges 10, 12, 14, 16, 18, 20 and 22 well stocked in my studio, with the 18-, 20- and 22-gauge spools getting the most use. I typically use 16- or 18-gauge wire to make jump rings, clasps and closures; 20-gauge for ear wires and wrapped loops; and 22-gauge for metal fibers that I use in wire wrapping and lashing. (We'll get to metal fibers in this chapter.)

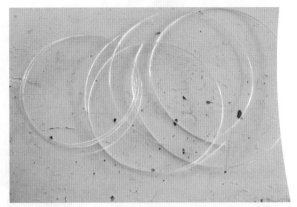

Various gauges of sterling silver wire

Metal sheet also comes in the same B&S unit of measurement, from the heaviest sheet being a 2-gauge all the way to a thin 30-gauge. When ordering sheet metal from a jewelry supply company, you will most likely purchase it in 6" or 12" (15cm or 30cm) widths. Copper and brass sheet metal—which you buy at your local hardware store—has a different standard of measurement for the tooling trade, but I often buy my base metals there because they are inexpensive and readily available. Many jewelers prefer to work with 18- and 20-gauge sheet metal, but I've found the best starting point is 22- or 24-gauge sterling silver and 24-gauge bronze, nickel or brass. These gauge metals are heavy enough for back plates and other structures while still being easily manipulated with shears, pliers and fingers.

Various gauges of bronze wire

Various metal sheets, from left to right: bronze, nickel, brass, copper, sterling silver and aluminum

cutting metal

To make metal jewelry, you will need to cut sheet metal into shapes as well as trim wire to various lengths. Sheet metal can be cut with a jeweler's saw or a good quality pair of shears. While most instructors insist metalworking education start from day one with the jeweler's saw, I freely admit I'm quite comfortable using my shears for basic shapes such as squares, rectangles, triangles and organic circles. That said, learning the jeweler's saw is definitely advantageous because it can cut almost any material. It's also nearly impossible to take your work to a finer level of craftsmanship without it.

Jeweler's Saw

A jeweler's saw is comprised of an adjustable frame with a thumbscrew at the top and bottom to clamp a saw blade, which is a thin strip of tool steel with a series of teeth running down one side. Blades come in various sizes, from 8/0 (the thinnest) down to 0 and then from 1 to 14 (the thickest), which refers to the size of the teeth. The most commonly used sizes for jewelry are 4/0, 3/0 and 2/0 for metal sheet ranging from 20-gauge to 24-gauge. Jeweler's saw blades come in packages of a dozen or more and are sold by the size. When first learning to saw, it's good to have extras on hand because blades can break easily until you get the hang of it.

To load the saw, sit at your worktable and hold the frame facing down toward the floor with the C-shaped opening facing up where the saw blade goes. Using your free hand, insert a blade into the top thumbscrew so the teeth of the blade are facing down and out, and tighten the wing nut to lock the blade into position.

Switch the saw frame to your dominant hand and brace the top end of the saw against the table's ledge and the handle against your abdomen. Lean into the table, creating a bit of tension in the frame, and insert the bottom end of the blade into the bottom thumbscrew, tightening the wing nut to lock it into place. Lean back to release the frame so the blade is strung taut. When you let go, pluck the blade. You should hear a melodic "ping" sound, which means it's ready for use.

To saw metal, you will also need a V-slotted bench pin that clamps onto your work bench. If you buy a bench pin without the V-slot, you will need to cut one into it before you work, so save yourself time by purchasing one already done for you. A bench pin is needed to support both the front and back of your metal as you saw.

Sit in your chair and position yourself directly in front of your bench pin. Line up your legs and body perpendicular to the bench pin and hold the loaded jeweler's saw loosely at a 90° angle in your dominant hand. Place your piece of metal so it's located over the V slot, hold the handle so it rests loosely in your hand and start your saw with a downward pull. After a few strokes, use your other hand to hold the metal securely as you saw by placing your middle and index fingers on top of the metal piece and your thumb underneath. Continue to saw up and down, letting the tension of the saw blade do the work. Let out a big breath of air and then breathe some more. Relax. I've learned that when I'm struggling with my jeweler's saw, it's because I'm moving too quickly and forcing this precision tool through sheet metal as if it were a common hacksaw.

Shears

Being a lifelong crafter, I love shears. They are sharp, quick and easy to use. But they do have their drawbacks; namely, they bend the metal as they cut and leave rough edges that absolutely must be smoothed out by filing. I used shears for a majority of the projects in this book for one simple reason: Many people are intimidated by the jeweler's saw. The fear is palpable enough that it keeps too many creative types who love making jewelry from the joys of metalworking.

Files

Whenever you use shears to cut metal, be sure to spend whatever time is necessary to file away sharp edges. My favorite two files are medium-cut, half-round and flat files I purchased at the hardware store. I use the round side of my half-round file for circles and curves and the flat side for straight cuts. I also have a set of jewelry needle files that I use to get into small areas or to smooth drill holes, etc. Filing works in one direction: away from you. To quickly file a straight edge, brace your cut piece of metal on your workbench or bench pin with your nondominant hand and file in long, smooth strokes. For small pieces, you can use a vise or wooden ring clamp to keep the metal in place as you file.

Because jewelry, and in particular metal jewelry, must be comfortable to wear, I almost always snip off the tiny tip of sharp corners and file them into a slightly rounded shape. I also finish my edges with a quick sanding of 320 or 400 grit wet/dry sandpaper or a couple of swipes of a ladies nail file.

Jeweler's saw and bench pin

Various shears and cutters, from left to right: aluminum snips, French shears, heavy-duty double flush cutters, wire cutters

Various files—from left to right: diamond needle flies in a set; steel half-round and precision-cut flat

Disc Cutter

Metalworking tools can be pricey. I believe it's perfectly acceptable at the beginning of a new hobby to buy entry-level quality tools. After your skills improve and you find yourself even more excited about making metal jewelry, I recommend stepping up your purchases and buying good tools, especially jewelry workhorses such as pliers and hammers. I know this is contrary to what many instructors teach. Why buy two sets of things when you can save time and money and buy the best to begin with? Although I agree with the reasoning, I've found people don't think this way when contemplating a new medium. They want to dive right in and not have the process cost a fortune.

However, there's one tool I think should be a lifetime purchase right from the beginning: a metal disc cutter set. Why? Because punching perfectly round circles out of metal is extremely satisfying, and the design options for earrings, necklaces, rings and bracelets are endless.

A good disc cutter made of carbon tool steel will cut incremental circles with a diameter of ⅛" to 1" (3mm to 1cm), and it will last forever.

The disc cutter tool is used in tandem with dapping tools—dapping blocks and dies, which create a concave or convex shape to metal discs.

To Use a Disc Cutter

1. Unscrew the center nut that holds the top and bottom sections of the cutter together until there's enough room between the two halves to slide in your metal sheet.

2. Place your sheet metal under the size hole you wish to punch and screw down the center nut so it holds the metal firmly in place.

3. Choose the circle punch die that corresponds to the diameter hole you selected and place it in the hole. Hold the disc cutter with your nondominant hand to keep it steady, and then using a standard hammer, strike a blow to the center of the die. It should go about halfway through. Strike the hammer one more time, which should be enough for the die to cut through, releasing a perfectly cut disc from the bottom of the cutter. Be sure you're working on a solid and stable work surface so the force of the hammer easily does the cutting.

4. Remove the excess sheet from the cutter.

Punches and Drills

When making metal jewelry, it's important to have tools that make holes. These tools can range from handheld punch pliers to a two-hole screw-down metal punch to a simple drill that you crank by hand. My 1.8 metal hole punch is a workhorse because it creates perfect holes for micro nuts and screws and other standard nail head rivets. Also, the two-hole screw punch is a handy dandy tool because it's strong enough to make holes in copper pennies and offers two hole sizes: a smaller 1.60mm and larger 2.30mm. All you have to do for this tool is decide the size hole you wish to make, slide your sheet metal into the slot and crank the top levers of the tool. For heavier gauge or harder metals such as bronze, you will need something with more power. This can be a rotary Dremel tool, a drill press or a flexible shaft, which comes with a foot pedal to control the speed. A standard trigger-type drill has too much torque and speed for working with smaller and softer pieces of metal, which makes it unsuitable for metalsmithing. All of the projects in this book use a standard size $\frac{1}{16}$" (2mm) drill bit that's readily available at hardware stores. (Be sure to purchase bits for metal and not wood.) I also love using my metal punch pliers because they are quick and easy and can easily go through 20-gauge sheet metal.

To properly drill a hole in metal, decide where you want your hole to be and place the tip of a center punch on the metal. Hammer a quick blow to the top of the center punch to make a small divot in the metal. This is necessary because the drill will "walk" across the metal, leaving gouges, unless you first create a pilot hole for the drill bit to grab onto. Holding the drill directly above the divot, place the bit into the divot and drill slowly straight down into the metal. Keeping the drill straight, rather than angled, ensures a clean hole and keeps drill bits from breaking. Drill slowly at first, increasing speed as the bit bites into the metal. You'll know if you're drilling correctly when you get nice long coils of metal coming out of the drilled hole. Small, sharp metal shards mean you're either drilling too fast or holding the bit at an angle, both of which take a toll on your tool. Always wear safety glasses and drill on a scrap piece of wood to protect your worktable.

Left: forming block, dapping blocks and dies
Right: disc cutter and dies

From left to right: 1.8 metal hole punch, handheld $\frac{1}{16}$" (2mm) punch, spring-loaded center punch, standard center punch

forging, stamping and forming metal

Forging is the displacement (spreading) of metal molecules by flattening metal with a hammer and anvil. It's one of the oldest known metalworking processes and is still a staple technique for artists creating metal jewelry. Stamping is akin to forging—still a displacement of metal—with a specific intent to leave a deliberate mark, be it letters for a word or a design that creates an image or pattern. And forming, or shaping, takes metal from a two-dimensional level to that of a third dimension by coercing it into curves, folds, coils, bends or any free-form shape. There is one tool that is instrumental in all of these tasks, and that is the hammer.

Hammers

The humble hammer is an essential tool on the metalsmith's bench. It's used for forging, stamping/texturing and forming metal, and there are many types of hammers for each of these primary tasks.

When using a hammer for any task, hold it at its "sweet spot" for proper metalworking, which is down closer to the end of the handle rather than the middle. Don't choke the handle toward the top, because it won't give you the tension you need to let the tool work properly. Also, don't use too tight of a grip, which can cause wrist strain.

In addition to forging, hammers are used to create various textures on metal. One of the simplest and most effective ways to do this is with a simple ball-peen hammer and a steel bench block. Some of my favorite earrings to make are metal circles punched from a disc cutter and texturized with ball-peen hammers. Another technique is to use the ball side of a chasing hammer to make light dimples around the edge of simple metal shapes, creating a deckled-edge look; you'll see me use that technique in some of the projects. And, if you desire something fancier than the basic ball-peen hammer, there are some great texture hammers available to make stripes, crosshatch marks, embossed and debossed dots, stars and more.

Various hammers, from left to right: rawhide mallet, standard dead-blow hammer with ball-peen end, brass hammer, chasing hammer

Forging

The simplest form of forging is that which is done on a piece of wire—striking it with the flat side of a heavy ball-peen hammer against either an anvil or steel bench block. But striking a piece of metal sheet will accomplish the same thing—the process of spreading out the metal. A by-product of all of this striking is what's known as work hardening.

With each blow of the hammer, you are work hardening your metal. When it becomes stiff and hard to bend, but you wish to still shape or form it, you will need to anneal the metal to reshape the molecules and soften it. Annealing can be done many times to the same piece of metal. Be sure to anneal before the forged metal becomes too brittle, or it will fissure and crack if you overwork it. You will know you've annealed properly when the metal has a black sooty firescale on it and it's butter soft. (See page 16 for more on annealing.)

To create a dimpled texture on your forged metal, use the ball-peen side of your hammer, striking a series of blows along the length of the piece to create a gorgeous hand-hammered look to the metal.

Texturizing hammers

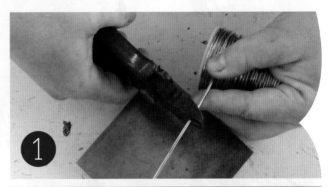

Forging Wire
1. Cut a length of wire—here I am using 12-gauge.

2. As you hammer, hit the metal with a hard blow, pushing the wire away from you so the blows lengthen the metal. This is called drawing out the metal. Your metal will naturally curl up as you forge it.

When you finish hammering one side, flip the wire over and do the same to the other side to flatten out the piece.

Texturing wire with a ball-peen hammer

Annealing

Each time you bend or hammer wire or a piece of metal, you are changing the metal's molecular structure, which is called work hardening. Metal goes from dead soft to half-hard to hard. If it's overworked beyond hard, it goes to spring hard and then eventually cracks or breaks. You can return its molecular structure to soft and malleable by annealing it with a torch. As a safety measure, have a pan of water next to your torch in order to quickly quench (cool) your metal after annealing it. It's good to get into the habit of always quenching immediately following any torch work, which includes drawing a bead or heat patina, as well as annealing. Annealing is an important process for metalworking, particularly when you are forging and texturizing—which you'll be doing in most of the projects in this book.

Sterling silver has a much lower melting point than bronze. When working with sterling silver, heat your metal only until it becomes a dull red, being sure to slowly but steadily move your torch back and forth over the metal, ensuring an even heating. If your sterling silver changes from a dull red to a cherry red, your metal is about to melt. Because bronze is a much harder alloy, its annealing and melting temperatures are higher. To anneal bronze, use the same technique of moving your torch back and forth over the metal, allowing it to come to a cherry red, but be careful to not take it to a bright orange state where it will melt. When drawing a bead on thinner-gauge wires, such as 20 to 22, work quickly with your torch, as these pieces of wire can be crispy fried in seconds with a hot torch such as oxygen/acetylene or MAPP gas. Using a good quality butane torch on thin wire is easier to control.

Annealing can be done over and over again on the same piece of metal to recondition work-hardened metal. This is especially helpful for projects like the Free-Form Forged Bangles (page 58). You can continue to add texture to your heavy-gauge wire and then soften the metal by annealing it in order to form the wire around either a bracelet or ring mandrel.

You will know that your metal has been properly annealed when it is soft enough to bend with your fingers, even heavy-gauge metal. It will also have a sooty residue on it called firescale.

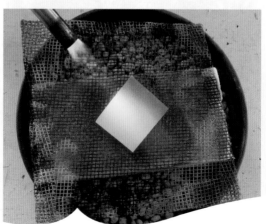

Firescale and Pickle

The easiest way to remove firescale is to gently drop your cooled piece of metal into a pickle bath, but you can also sand it off with a piece of sandpaper or extra-fine steel wool. Pickle is a mild cleaning solution for metal that works best warm, which is why most jewelers have it in a slow cooker in their studios. Pickle for sterling silver is sodium bisulfate, sold in a dry granular mix, but you can mix up a greener solution at home with 1 tablespoon of salt for every cup of water. There is a different pickle solution for brass, bronze and nickel called 50/50, with a homemade solution being one part regular sodium bisulfate pickle to one part hydrogen peroxide, which you can buy at the drug store. These metals will often get a slight pink tint to them when soaked in regular pickle. If you plan to add patina, you can often skip the step of using a 50/50 pickle with the base metals, but if you plan to buff your finished pieces to a high shine, it's worth the extra step.

When gently placing your metal into pickle to clean off the oxidation of firescale, always use copper tongs. Keep the temperature on your slow cooker turned down low, never letting it boil over, because commercial solutions can cause fumes if overheated. Wearing safety eyewear is also recommended in case the liquid splashes. Fresh pickle will usually work quickly—five minutes or less—whereas older pickle can take up to thirty minutes or more. When the pickle stops removing firescale or turns blue, it's spent and will need to be neutralized with baking soda and disposed of properly. I keep my used pickle in a recycled plastic tub and turn it in during my city's hazardous waste collection days. Please never pour your used pickle, patinas or etching chemicals down the drain, and if you have young children at home, store all of your chemicals up high and out of reach.

Paddling

Paddling the end of a piece of wire refers to a process of forging it so that it is flat on one (or both) end(s) and can then act as a headpin or the end can be rolled with round-nose pliers to create a loop.

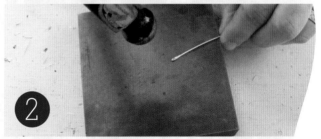

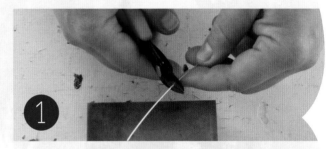

Making a Paddle

1. Cut a length of wire with flush cutters.

2. Using a ball-peen hammer, spread out the end of the wire by sweeping over it as you hit it on a steel block. This flattens it and creates a paddle shape. The "spoon" or paddle shape should be about ¼" (6mm) in length.

3. This creates a stopper for a bead, which is an alternative for a headpin.

Dapping

A dapping block is especially well suited for metal discs that you've punched out with your disc cutter. A dapping block takes shapes—primarily circles—from a flat piece of metal to a lovely, three-dimensional, domed form.

You can buy a dapping block at jewelry supply stores in either polished steel or wood. If you plan to do a lot of dapping, you might consider buying the steel one from the get-go, because this is another lifetime metalworking tool. The dapping cube has a series of round cavities that perfectly fit the dapping punches, which are a series of dies with a ball on top.

You can spend a lot of time dapping the same disc, graduating to smaller and smaller holes and punches until the metal moves upward into a pod shape. It's really cool to see the forging and forming action of metal and tools this way, which is called upsetting the metal because the length is changed by squeezing it over a die.

Stamping Metal

Being able to personalize your work with words, names or patterns is one of the most appealing things about learning to make your own metal jewelry. Steel alphabet- and number-set stamps are easy to find and are another tool investment that will last a lifetime.

To get a good impression, work on a solid surface. I have an old butcher-block table that I do my forging, texturizing and stamping on. Your steel block needs to sit flat on the surface with no cushion or pounding mat underneath it. (Yes, this means it will be noisier, but you will get a much nicer result.)

Use your standard heavy hammer, holding it in your dominant hand, and pick up a metal stamp with your other hand, holding the stamp right in the middle with your thumb and first two fingers and your hand resting on the block for additional stabilization. Press the stamp into the metal (softer metals such as copper and dead soft sterling silver work beautifully), and strike it with the hammer.

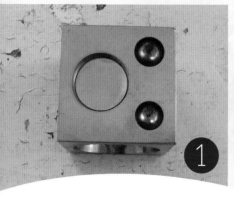

Dapping

1. Take a metal disc and place it into a cup on the block that is larger than the disc.

2. Use the corresponding die and place it over the metal. Using a standard dead-blow hammer or a heavy mallet, hammer the top of the die to begin forming a dome in the metal. Move your hammer around the top of the die so the metal is evenly displaced to create a nice dome. As the disc domes, move it to a smaller cavity and use a smaller corresponding punch. Continue to dap your disc to your aesthetic.

3. Here is the finished bowl.

Because stamping actually displaces the metal so it forms up and around the die, the hammer needs to hit the top of the stamp dead center with enough force to make a decent impression. Attempt to hit the stamp with enough force the first time so it makes a clear impression. If you feel like you hit it off center, do not pick up the metal stamp. Hold it still exactly where it is and then slightly tilt it forward and hit it again. If you pick up your stamp, you will probably not get it back into the same groove, and a second hit will cause a shadowed or double-impression imprint.

It can be difficult to correctly center and line up a word. One of the easiest ways to ensure a word is centered where you want it is to find the center of the metal and the center of the word and start there. For example, if I were to stamp the word "dream," I would stamp the letter E first and then work to the right, stamping A and then M. I'd then go back and stamp the R and, finally, the D.

Don't forget that your letter stamps can also be used to make repeating patterns as well, like a series of Xs to look like cross-stitch or Os for a circle border. Go one step further with those Os and use your center punch to add another dot in the center of the O for a nice effect, punching it one way for an embossed look or turning it for a debossed look. Oh, the possibilities!

Once you start playing around with an alphabet stamp set, you'll probably look to purchase some design stamps as well. These are really fun to use for borders and to create random patterns on your pieces, such as the falling leaves used on the copper band in my Cold Enamel Ring project on page 74.

Mandrels

Forming and shaping a piece of wire or metal sheet can be easily accomplished after the metal has been forged and annealed. You can hand-form pieces for a sculptural aesthetic, but most metal jewelry is shaped around specific tools called mandrels. There are ring mandrels, bracelet mandrels and so on. Most silversmithing mandrels are made from highly polished steel, but wooden ones are also available. I often use unconventional objects around my studio as forming tools, including glue bottles, wooden dowel rods, markers, baseball bats, etc.

When shaping around a mandrel, the easiest way to begin is to place your forged and annealed wire or metal sheet on the mandrel and begin in the middle to start gently hand-shaping the metal around the curve. After you have the shape started, use a rubber or rawhide mallet to gently tap the metal, following the curve of the mandrel. This will ensure a nice, consistently rounded shape. Follow this process for rings, bracelets or round links when making your own chain.

Various mandrels, from left to right: wooden dowels, ring mandrel, bench pin bracelet mandrel, wooden bracelet mandrel

Pliers

Pliers are absolutely necessary for all types of jewelry making. Fortunately, you can perform most techniques with a good set of three pliers and a pair of wire cutters. You will want to purchase a quality pair of round-nose pliers. I prefer having both short and long round-nose pliers to work with. You'll also need a pair of chain-nose pliers and a pair of flat-nose pliers. These are essential tools for opening and closing jump rings and crimping wire after you make wrapped loops to ensure there are no sharp, protruding wires. I've also found a pair of nylon jaw pliers to be essential in wireworking, as they will smooth kinked wire and also work-harden it slightly when running a piece of wire through the jaws. For torch work, you will need a junk pair of long needle-nose pliers to safely grasp wire and metal when dipping them into a flame or removing them from the pumice stone or metal tripods that are used for annealing. My needle-nose pliers are only used with my torch. I have quite a collection of basic and specialty pliers. Over the years, I've bought ergonomic ones, economical ones and expensive ones; I just can't seem to get enough. However, the ones pictured here are what I turn to every time I work.

Various pliers, clockwise from top: round-nose, chain-nose, nylon jaw, needle-nose, long round-nose, flat-nose

Working Wire

The projects in this book all take on some sort of wirework in which shaping wire into loops with the help of pliers is employed. The organic wire work that I do is very forgiving and "messy," but if you prefer a neater look, this is easily accomplished; it just takes a bit of practice to get your groove down.

Making an organic loop is a lesson in abundance of material and free-form wrapping. It's wonderful for those of us who like to eyeball things, instead of needing exact measurements. To make an organic loop, use a least two or three times more wire than you would for a normal wrapped loop. Use your round-nose pliers to make a loop, crossing the larger end of the wire over the smaller one and wrapping it around and around until you either run out of wire or achieve the look you want. To keep the wire from becoming a big ball, be sure to wind your wire end up and down, creating a more oval wrap, rather than a round shape.

Simple Wire Loop

1. Grasp the end of the wire in a pair of round-nose pliers.

2. Bring the wire around the cone shape of the pliers until it makes a complete circle.

3. Move the tip of the pliers to the outside of the loop and "break the neck" by bending the loop back a bit so the loop is centered over the remaining length of wire.

4. Here is the finished loop.

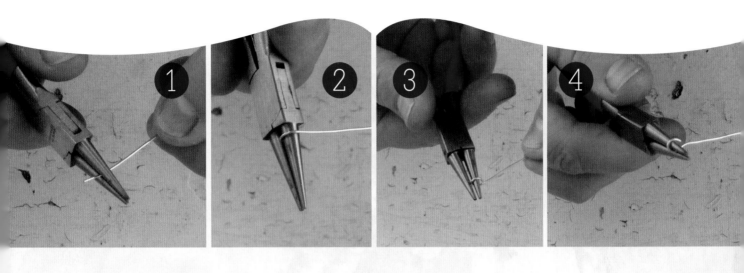

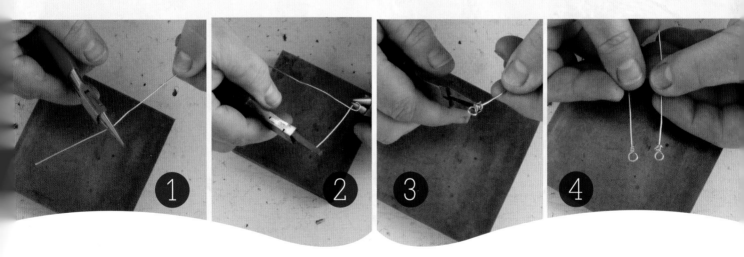

Wrapped Wire Loop

1. Grasp the wire about 2" (5cm) from the end with the middle of the pliers.

2. Roll the wire all the way around and cross it over itself.

3. Hold the pliers in your nondominant hand, and with a second pair of pliers, grab the short end of the wire and wrap this tail around the wire at the base of the loop about three times. This can be "messy" and need not be perfect. Often, I just use my fingers to wrap the wire. Trim the excess wire with flush cutters. Crimp the end with pliers to keep it from being sharp.

4. Alternatively, you might want your wraps to be neat and tidy (not my style!). Here is a look at the organic wrap and the neat-and-tidy wrap.

etching metal, adding patinas and finishing

Texture plays an important role in my art. To me, things are much more interesting when the juxtaposition of disparate elements play off each other, such as hard edges and soft ribbons or girlie bling paired with grunge. Incorporating etching and/or patina techniques helps me achieve this aesthetic. I also believe finishing techniques, such as polishing and shining your jewelry, displays professionalism and dedication to craftsmanship.

Etching

Another way to get sophisticated texture onto metal is to chemically etch it. Mixed-media artists working in a variety of mediums have embraced the technique I want to share with you here. It's really quite fun to use rubber stamp images and transfer them to metal permanently through a chemical process. Most jewelers use ferric chloride—an etchant used in the electronics industry to etch copper circuit boards—for this technique. Unfortunately, where I live, ferric chloride is not readily accessible. Therefore, I use a combination of two parts common 3% hydrogen peroxide to one part muriatic acid, which is sold alongside pool chemicals. This etching solution does not work on sterling silver but will work nicely on copper, brass, bronze and nickel silver. Unlike ferric chloride that can be used multiple times, this chemical combination loses its strength with no more than a couple of etches. Pour baking soda into the plastic container when you are finished etching so you can neutralize the etchant and dispose of it properly during your city or town's hazardous waste drop-off days.

Etching Metal

1. To etch metal, first clean your piece of metal using acetone. Any oils from your hands or body will cause a resist so the etchant can't penetrate the metal. Apply a black solvent-based ink, such as StazOn, to your rubber stamp image.

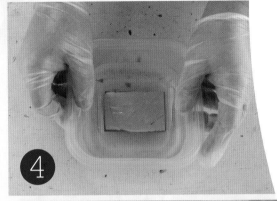

2. Apply your metal to the stamp. I've found I get a sharper stamp when I apply the metal to the stamp, rather than the other way around. If my piece is flat, I put my inked rubber stamp on my wood table facing up and then gently place my metal onto the stamp, gently pressing on the metal for an even stamp.

3. Place the metal onto a firebrick or in an annealing pan filled with pumice stone and use a craft heat gun made for stamping to heat-set the ink. Let the metal cool completely before moving to the next step.

4. As a safety precaution, don disposable latex gloves before working with chemicals. Fill a disposable plastic or glass container with two parts hydrogen peroxide to one part muriatic acid. Attach your metal to a long strip of plastic packing tape and place the stamped metal facedown into the solution, taping the ends on either side to the container.

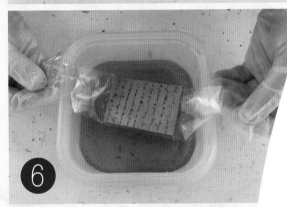

5. The solution will turn blue almost immediately. A fresh etch with this type of etchant solution will take a minimum of two hours and as much as six hours. If you leave it in the solution overnight, it will eat away the metal and molder the edges—a look I sometimes do on purpose to achieve an organic-looking edge. The trade-off, though, is a fuzzier image rather than a crisp etch.

6. Wear gloves when removing your etched metal from the solution. Neutralize the etched metal immediately in baking soda.

7. Then use an old toothbrush or a green kitchen sponge with water to remove any remaining ink.

Patinas

This is just a personal opinion, but if you're going to take the extra steps to add lovely texture to your metal with hammers, metal stamps, etched designs, etc., then why not show off all its surface goodness by adding patina to your metalwork? I know some people like their metal shiny, and sometimes I keep my metals—especially sterling silver—pristine, but more often than not, I tend to prefer a heavily patinated look to highlight all the texture. There are a number of ways to add patina to metals, ranging from natural solutions of ammonia and salt (gorgeous on brass) to commercially available ones such as liver of sulfur. For the projects here, I use liquid liver of sulfur in hot water for sterling silver and Jax Brown for bronze, brass and copper. I also use Jax Green for a verdigris finish on brass and bronze, but the patinated metal needs to be sealed so it doesn't flake off with wear. Most commercially available patina solutions contain toxic warnings, so always use appropriate precautions. You can also get a gorgeous natural patina on bronze and copper by applying heat to it with a torch.

LIVER OF SULFUR

To use liver of sulfur, mix a small amount of liquid or a few solid chunks in hot water in a plastic disposable container. Liver of sulfur smells like rotten eggs, so use it in a well-ventilated area. It works best warm. Place your textured metal into the container and wait for it to turn black. Pull your metal piece from the container with a pair of old tweezers and rinse the metal under cold water to stop the oxidation process. Polish with a piece of fine steel wool or a green kitchen sponge. If you want a high-shine finish, use a rotary tumbler with stainless steel shot if you have one, or a polishing wheel on your flexible shaft or rotary tool. The process is the same for Jax patinas.

HYDROCHLORIC ACID

To use a fast-acting hydrochloric acid solution such as Griffith Silver Black, dip a paintbrush into the patina solution and paint a thin layer onto your metal. It will work almost instantly. Rinse in cold water and then polish to leave the black in the recessed areas and buff out the highlights.

GILDER'S PASTE

Another way to add patina is with an oil-based gilder's paste that looks like shoe polish. What I like about gilder's paste is that once applied to metal, it adheres permanently and doesn't need to be sealed. It also comes in a rainbow of luscious colors. Gilder's paste was traditionally used for decorative finishes, such as gilding iron lampposts and gates, so it holds up quite well on metal jewelry.

Polishing and Finishing

Finishing jewelry is an art form in and of itself. Many studio jewelers buff their pieces to a high shine and work diligently at it with a series of buffing wheels, tools and compounds. Most of the projects here use a simple polishing technique of buffing the metal with either a piece of extra-fine steel wool or a green kitchen scrub. I also have a couple of small polishing wheel attachments that work with my flexible shaft that I use whenever black patina settles deeply into crevices, like on rings or around bezels.

A rotary tumbler is a nifty tool to eventually purchase for your studio, because it makes quick work of polishing pieces to a high shine and also work-hardens jewelry as it polishes. For jewelry, you will want to buy stainless steel shot, the kind with a mixture of shapes including balls, pins and diagonals to work into all types of crevices. Put it on your tool wish list and purchase it when you can. Looking for a used one? Search under Lapidary on craigslist and eBay. Sometimes gently-used tumblers can be bought for a song!

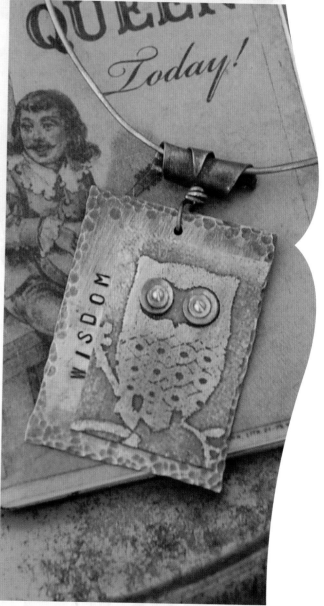

25

making metal attachments

Some of the most important skills you'll learn when it comes to creating your own jewelry components is how to attach the pieces and parts together so they're not only beautiful but strong and secure.

One of the most eloquent ways of attaching components is with cold connection techniques, meaning there is no heat such as soldering or glue involved in the joining of two or more pieces of metal. There are a lot of cold-join techniques, but I've chosen to focus on some of the most basic. These include eyelets, nuts and screws and nail-head rivets. Another expressive form of connection is wire wrapping, which I use on almost everything I make because it lends an interesting, organic look to my finished pieces.

Nuts and Screws and Micro Bolts

Trust me when I say these are just the greatest little invention. There are two sizes that I use: long and short micro bolts and nuts—both with a 1/16" (2mm) shank so they perfectly fit my 1/16" (2mm) drill bit or hole-punch pliers. The long ones build up height and provide a sturdy attachment, as seen in the Cold Enamel Ring (page 74) and Spinner Ring (page 78) projects. The tiny ones are great for joining shallow pieces of metal, like the dapped eyes on the Etched Owl Pendant (page 100).

To use the nuts and screws, thread the shank through a hole in a piece of metal and then twist down the corresponding nut using your fingers. Use your flat-nose pliers, or chain-nose in tight spots, when you get to the end to tighten the nut so it's completely secure.

Here's a great tip given to me by my fellow mixed-media artist and jeweler Barbe Saint John. To secure the nut forever, ensuring it won't ever work itself loose, add a tiny dot of thick, clear resin to the top of the piece. You will need to use a jeweler's-grade resin because others that aren't self-doming will slide right off the nut and down the shank, making a mess. Epoxy resin is much stronger and more permanent than glue.

Eyelets

Eyelets have traditionally been used in paper arts, but recently they have been making an appearance in metal jewelry as an easy cold connection. Look for tiny 1/16" (2mm) eyelets—more suited to jewelry—rather than the commonly found 1/8" (3mm) size for paper. Also, it's good to purchase them in short, medium and long to fit the metal components you're stacking. Unlike paper where a little wiggle room is okay, improperly fitting metal components will not hold up to normal jewelry wear.

To set an eyelet in a metal blank or sheet metal shape, punch or drill a hole in the metal. Join your metal pieces together by lining up the holes and insert the eyelet into the hole so the round, flat side is flush with one side of the metal. Turn the work over so the eyelet front is face down on your steel bench block and the shank is facing up. Insert a center punch tool into the tube part of the hole. Gently hit the top of the center punch with a hammer, tilting it ever so slightly outward as you hit to create a flared end. Move your punch, tilting outward in a new direction (north, south, east and west) as you hammer. Remove your center punch, and you should see a nicely flared circle where the top of the eyelet shank is curling over onto itself. If you have a riveting hammer, switch to it now and gently hammer down the eyelet. If you don't have a riveting hammer, switch to the ball end of your ball-peen hammer to finish setting the eyelet.

With practice, you'll set your eyelet on the back of your metal so it looks as smooth as the commercially finished side on the front. There are eyelet-setting tools used in paper crafting that will also set eyelets into metal. The only problem is that many of these are not suited for the 1/16" (2mm) size.

Rivets

There are a number of different methods for riveting,—a super-strong form of cold connection. Silversmiths and studio jewelers often make their own rivets out of wire and rivet them into place. These rivets are usually set into the metal so there is a small mushroom-shaped top, which is spread out over the metal for a secure attachment. Wire rivets can also be set flush into the metal, and they are often called blind rivets because they're made to be virtually unnoticeable. Other times, the metalsmith will draw a bead on the end of the wire (see page 31) to create a nail-head rivet, which is used both as a connection and a design element.

The simplest method to begin riveting is to learn to use a manufactured nail-head rivet. The rivets look like a nail, with a wide flat head at the top and a straight metal shaft extending from the center. The most important part about riveting is a proper fit. The size of the rivet and the size of the hole must fit together very snugly. If the hole is even slightly larger, the rivet will slide right through and not hold properly. There are many types of manufactured nail-head rivets to choose from: decorative, numbered nails; hammered-metal-looking upholstery tacks; even the screw part of the nut-and-screw attachment can be used as a rivet. Anything with a rounded or flat top and a metal shank can potentially be used to rivet metal jewelry.

To set a rivet, drill or punch a hole in your metal whose diameter perfectly matches that of the rivet shaft. Inset the rivet into the hole and ensure a tight fit at the rounded top. Using a pair of heavy-duty flush cutters, cut the metal shaft so only a small amount of wire is left to hammer. Place the top side of your nail-head rivet onto your steel bench block and, using either a small riveting hammer or the ball end of your ball-peen hammer, gently tap the metal shaft. Pivot the head of your hammer slightly outward and gently tap in all directions—north, south, east and west—in order to get a rounded head to your wire. The top should look like a mushroom or nail head when finished.

Wire Wrapping

Another effective cold connection is wire wrapping two components together with thinner wire, such 20-gauge or 22-gauge. Making a loop (see page 21) is one of the first forms of connection you'll learn when making your own jewelry, because loops are probably the most basic cold connection after opening and closing jump rings. The look of messy wraps is currently popular among mixed-media jewelry artists. One of the original creators of this look is Nina Bagley, who made and taught what she called the Nina Knot at mixed-media art retreats several years ago. I prefer to call these heavily wrapped loops organic rather than messy, but I use them almost exclusively in my connections because they are my exact aesthetic.

A final note on the value of wire wrapping as an attachment: When you directly wrap your loops together to create a link, you create a much stronger connection of closed metal onto closed metal rather than using jump rings that can work their way open during wear.

Metal Fibers

You can create a strong piece of metal for cold connection by drawing a bead (making these is explained on page 31) on both ends of a piece of wire and wrapping them around fibers, velvet, cording, lace and nontraditional materials for jewelry. They are a lovely decorative element as well. I use them in contrasting metals to add design details to pieces. If you have a bad loop that's lopsided or just not quite right, you can wrap a metal fiber around it just like a little wire bandage and nobody will ever notice the mistake. Add patina to your metal fibers to bring out the wrapped highlights and lowlights of the metal wire.

Lashing

You can also use thin-gauge wire to lash pieces of metal together for another cold join, such as the technique I did on the Dapped Circles Necklace (page 114) to join the metal focal element to the silk ribbon necklace. I also used lashing as a decorative element in the Wire-Stitched Pendant (page 108) to create a metal-stitched design. To use lashing, simply drill holes into metal and then sew or knot with a 24-gauge or higher metal wire to join the pieces together.

torching and soldering

You can make a lot of metal jewelry by using strictly cold connections. However, just as the jeweler's saw can expand your potential for more intricate shapes and designs, getting comfortable with a torch is a necessary step to take your metalsmithing skills to another level.

For beginners, a straightforward torch is a good-quality butane torch, such as one used to make crème brûlée. Be careful, however, to not buy an inexpensive one because it won't get hot enough for jewelry making. Even for drawing a bead on something like 22-gauge bronze wire, you will need a butane torch that heats to at least 2400° (1316° C). A hot butane torch can be found at many jewelry supply stores, usually as a beginning solder kit, or at high-end cooking stores. It can be advantageous to buy the solder kit because it comes with not only a torch, but also a Solderite board, solder, interlocking tweezers, a titanium pick, flux and often an instructional DVD.

My butane torch doesn't usually get a lot of action in my studio, because I prefer using a BenzOmatic 5-foot hose torch with a quick-start on/off trigger attached to a MAPP gas canister. I bought this torch for around $50 at my local home improvement store, as well as the fuel. I prefer the "Big Boy" canisters, as they sit a little more solidly. Just to be on the safe side, it's best to duct tape your MAPP gas canister to the table leg while you work so it doesn't tip over. I use this torch for drawing beads on my wire and annealing metals. Plumber torches are noisy, and you must take care when working with them to prevent accidents and burns. Keep your torch on only long enough to get the job accomplished in an effort to not fill your studio with too many gas fumes. Consider good ventilation, opening a window whenever possible.

Most metalsmiths and studio jewelers have either an oxygen/acetylene or a propane/acetylene torch set-up. I have yet to make this kind of purchase because, so far, I'm quite happy with my hardware store variety.

Soldering

There are various types of solder—paste solders in a tube, wire solder and sheet solders. Solder comes in hard, medium, easy and extra easy (referring to their melting temperatures). With the exception of paste solders, which already have flux built into the mixture, all solder must be used in conjunction with flux. Flux forms a protective film that keeps the air away from the metal, thereby allowing the solder to flow into the joins of metal.

The most important thing to keep in mind when soldering is that your metal must be squeaky clean. It's best to pickle all of your pieces, prior to soldering, when you're done shaping them. (See more about pickling on page 17). Any oil or grease on your fingers will transfer to the metal and can cause a resist, keeping the flux and solder from sticking to the metal.

To use paste silver solder, first align your metals so they fit perfectly together with no overlap and no gaps. Solder will never actually *fill* gaps; it will only flow into the tight-fitting spaces between the metal pieces. Squeeze out small balls of solder paste to the metal join. Transfer the piece to a Solderite board and turn on your torch.

Warm up your metal by gently and slowly moving your torch around the area of your piece, farthest away from the paste solder. Watch the metal for a color change, which indicates it's heating up. When the metal starts to glow, redirect your torch to the seam with the paste solder, which will flare up. Keep a gentle and steady flame on the join. You should see the solder melt quickly and start to flow into and across the join. Pull the torch away when you see the solder flow. Let it cool a moment and then use tweezers to flip the piece over; heat the solder up quickly to make it flow again to ensure an even seam. Let the piece cool and then place in pickle to clean the oxidation.

A Solderite board is great for paste solder because it doesn't retain heat. A firebrick or an annealing pan filled with pumice stone both retain heat, can melt the solder off too quickly. The latter is preferable when using wire or sheet solder, particularly in medium or hard.

Drawing a Bead on Wire

Drawing a bead on the end of a wire is one of the first torch techniques to learn when making jewelry. It's so simple and useful! When you dip the end of a piece of wire into the blue part of the flame, the wire will heat up and melt, curling in on itself, creating a little ball. These wires make the perfect headpins on which to thread washers, crystal beads and pearls. When you

draw a bead at both ends, you create what I refer to as a "**metal fiber**." I think these wires are just about the most useful thing in the world for cold-connection wire wrapping and as a design element.

Drawing a Bead

1. Using a pair of needle-nose pliers reserved for torch work, hold a length of wire in the propane flame. The tip of the wire should be at the tip of the blue part of the flame.

2. Hold it until the wire starts to melt and draws up into a small bead. A gut reaction is to pull the wire from the flame the moment the ball begins to form, but waiting a beat longer allows the heated metal to make a nice round ball.

3. When you have a nice ball, remove the wire from the flame. Be careful not to wait too long or the ball will fall off. It's a delicate balance!

4. To make a metal fiber, draw a bead on the other end of the wire as well.

31

making basic jewelry findings

Living in a small town for many years inspired a lot of "make it work" moments in my studio. I find it both practical and economical to always have wire and metal sheet well stocked in my studio. Not being able to run to my local bead store at a moment's notice encouraged me to learn how to make all of my own findings, from jump rings and ear wires to clasps and closures. Now, I prefer to create almost everything by hand so that my components are part of my art-making process and also my designs.

Jump Rings

One of the best things about making your own jump rings is that you can make any size you want, and you can always make them to match the rest of your project by using your choice of wire. The secret to making tight-fitting rings is to file the ends of the wire flat after you've snipped the rings off the coil.

  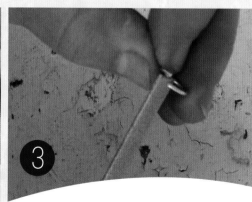

Making Jump Rings

1. Create a coil by wrapping a length of wire around a mandrel.

2. Remove the coil from the mandrel and snip apart individual rings using flush cutters.

3. File the beveled end of the ring to make it flat.

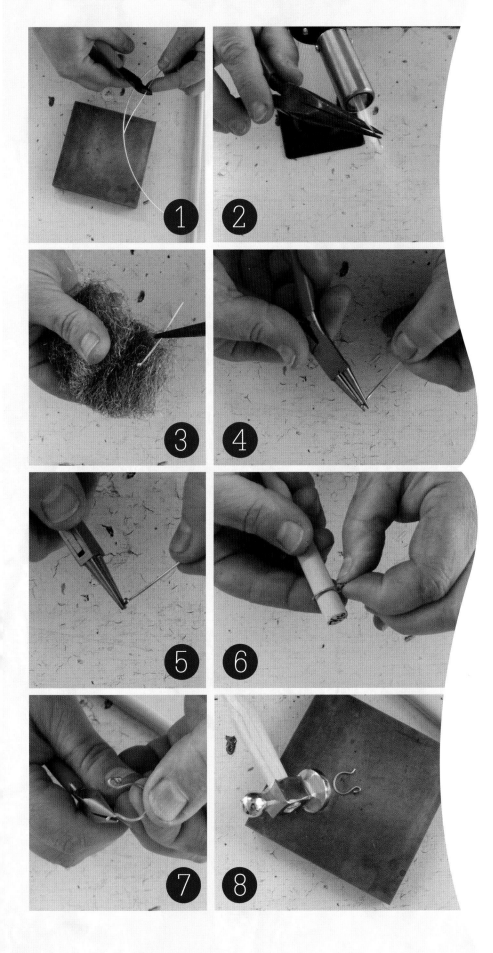

French Ear Wire

Another very easy finding to make is an ear wire. If you have sensitive ears, consider sticking to sterling silver wire. Experiment with different sized dowels to create your favorite look. The standard gauge for ear wires is 20-gauge.

French Ear Wire

1. Cut a 2" (5cm) length of wire.

2. Draw a bead on one end.

3. Remove the firescale with steel wool.

4. Create a little hook on the ball end of the wire using the end of your round-nose pliers.

5. Bend the loop back a bit to center it over the remaining length of wire.

6. Wrap the remaining wire in the opposite direction around a ½" (13mm) or 7/16" (22mm) mandrel.

7. Curl the end of the wire up just a bit.

8. Work-harden the ear wires in the center portion of the curve—just a bit—on a steel block.

Toggle Clasp

When creating your own toggle clasp, you may need to play around with the diameter of the loop and the length of the toggle. Ideally, the toggle is latched through the loop easily, but not so easily that it falls back through and your necklace falls off. I recommend always starting with the toggle and then creating a loop to fit, rather than the other way around.

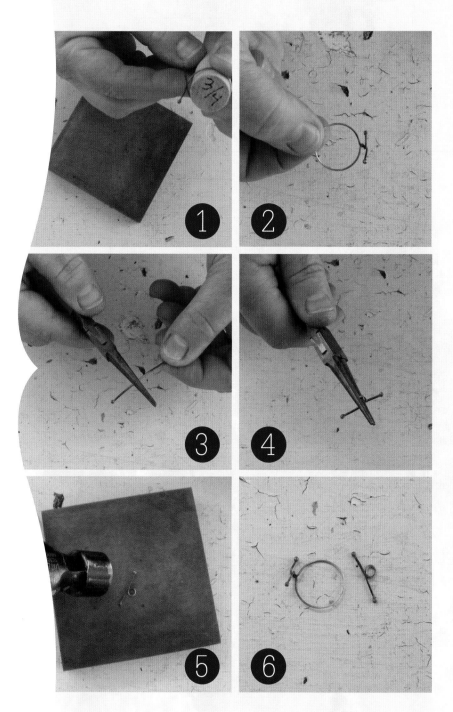

Toggle Clasp

1. To make the loop end of the toggle, wrap a metal fiber around a ¾" (19mm) dowel.

2. Twist the ends together where they meet.

3. Work-harden the loop, being careful not to smash the beads. To make the toggle end, cut a 1½" (4cm) piece of wire and make a metal fiber. Remove the firescale with some steel wool. Grasp the fiber in the center with the round-nose pliers.

4. Make a center loop, crossing the wires.

5. Work-harden the toggle a bit.

6. Here is the completed clasp.

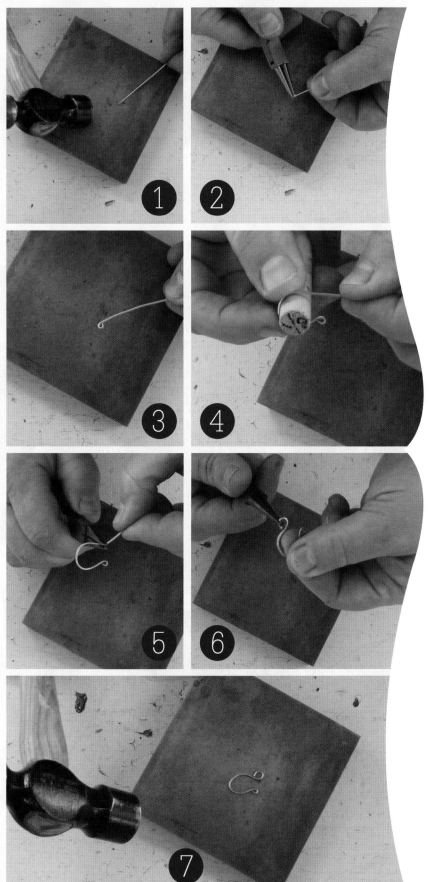

Shepherd's Hook Clasp

The shepherd's hook is a different kind of clasp, and one thing I like about the hook is that it can easily latch onto the end of a chain—no additional hardware necessary.

Shepherd's Hook Clasp

1. Cut a length of wire to about 2" (5cm) and create a paddle on one end of it.

2. Grasp the paddle with the end of the round-nose pliers.

3. Roll the wire around the pliers to make a complete loop.

4. Wrap the remaining wire around a pen or ½" (13mm) dowel in the opposite direction of the little loop.

5. Break the neck of the hook by bending it back a bit.

6. Use round-nose pliers to make a final loop on the other end of the wire, creating an S shape.

7. Hammer the finished clasp a bit to work-harden it.

metal jewelry projects

Now, as promised, onto the fun part—
making metal jewelry! In this section,
you'll find there are lots of new techniques
to try that will build on the basic
skills already introduced in the Metal
Fundamentals section. You'll learn cold-
join attachments such as riveting and
working with micro bolts. You'll also learn
how to use cool tools such as doming
and forming blocks, as well as ring and
bracelet mandrels. You'll also be working
with some unconventional materials such
as fibers and "found" objects. The basic
metalsmithing techniques introduced in
these beginning to intermediate jewelry-
making projects will sharpen your skills
quickly and enjoyably. No tedious lectures
or broken saw blades for you!

metal pin and earrings

In my experience, silversmith instruction always seem to begin with making a ring. Also from my experience, the *easiest* projects to start with are earrings. Sure, you have to make two of everything, but repetition is a key to success. Just for fun, I decided to start the projects with a completely organic, no-rhyme-or-reason, wire pin as a beginning exercise in loosing up your fingers and getting comfortable with pliers and mandrels. Every great pianist has to warm up her fingers before she begins her symphony. It's no different with metalworking.

free-form shawl pin

One of my favorite techniques in jewelry making is wire wrapping. The idea for this free-form shawl pin came to me one day after making a necklace bail with lots of loops and bends to the wire. I decided to take a long piece of wire to see if I could make a single sculptural piece, and this was born. My first attempt was with a thinner piece of 20-gauge bronze wire, but I quickly switched to 16-gauge to give the design more substance. Dead-soft sterling silver is a dream to work with for this technique.

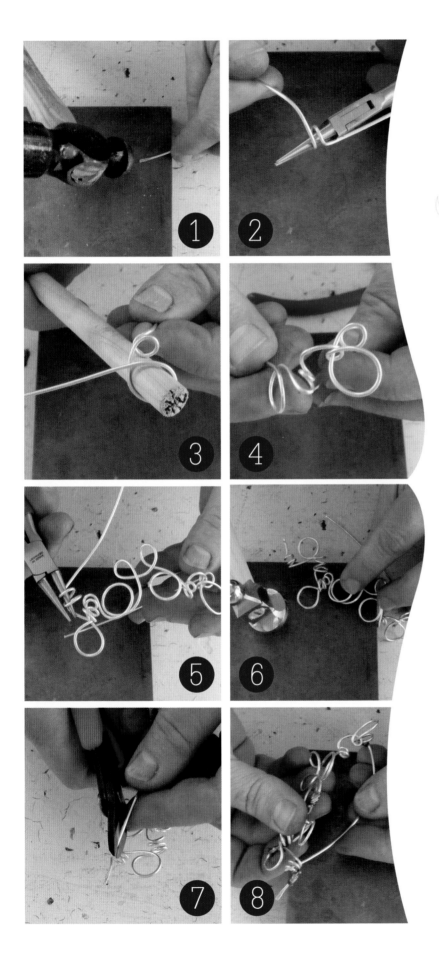

Tools

wire cutters

ball-peen hammer

flat-nose pliers

round-nose pliers

small wooden dowels

file

Materials

16-gauge wire, sterling silver

metal fibers made from 22-gauge
wire, bronze

1. Cut a 24" (61cm) length of 16-gauge
sterling silver wire. Using a ball-peen hammer,
flatten one end and make a paddle on it (see
page 17).

2. Use flat-nose pliers to create a bend, at
about 4" (10cm) from the opposite end.
Create a loop just before the bend, using
round-nose pliers.

3. Now create some larger loops using
a dowel.

4. Continue alternating loop sizes between the
pliers and assorted dowel sizes.

5. This is completely organic, and there is no
rhyme or reason to the number or direction of
the loops—do whatever looks good to you.

6. Work harden some of the larger loops.

7. Use your hands to shape the fibula so that
it will easily go into one of the small loops.
Cut the end of the wire at an angle, creating a
point. (File the end to smooth the metal burrs
and further sharpen the point.)

8. Wrap a few metal fibers around random
sections of the pin to create some visual inter-
est. Latch the point through one of the smaller
loops to close.

chased earrings

My grandmother used to tell me that when I wanted to learn a new skill all I had to do was "begin at the beginning." As a child, I would look at her quizzically, thinking, "Huh?" Today I understand what she meant. Start simple and don't tackle too much at once. These earrings are good starting point to learn how metal moves when you chase it with a hammer.

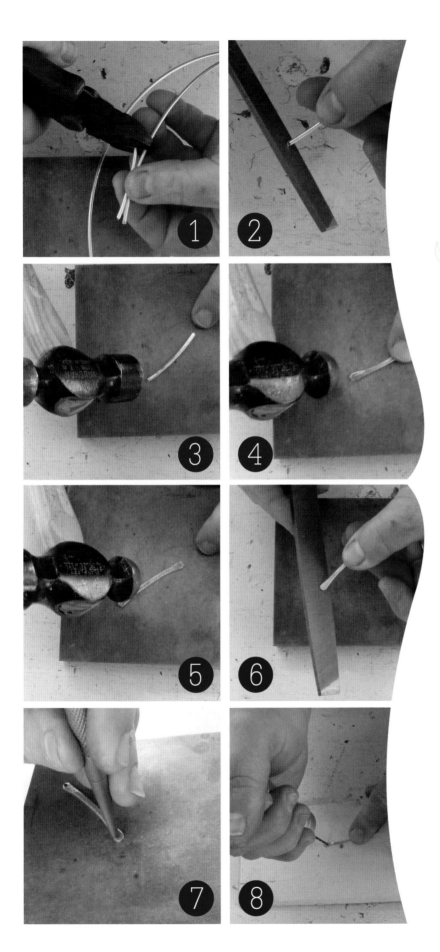

Tools

heavy-duty flush cutters

file

ball-peen hammer

center punch

hole punch, 1/16" (2mm) or drill

round-nose pliers

wire snips

steel wool

Materials

12-gauge wire, sterling silver

20-gauge wire, sterling silver

22-gauge wire, sterling silver

crystal beads

liver of sulfur

1. Using flush cutters, cut two 2" (5cm) lengths of 12-gauge sterling silver, dead soft round wire.

2. File both ends of both pieces to remove any burrs, making the ends flat.

3. Hammer both pieces of wire so they are fairly flat. Keep the natural curve of the wire; don't worry about making the pieces straight.

4. Flare out the ends on both pieces by hammering further with the ball end of the hammer, making paddles.

5. Create texture on the wires using the ball end of the hammer.

6. Use a file to smooth and round out the paddle shapes.

7. Use a center punch to mark for one hole in both ends of both wires.

8. Drill a tiny hole at each divot, using a drill or a punch. If you use a drill, be sure to drill into a piece of scrap wood.

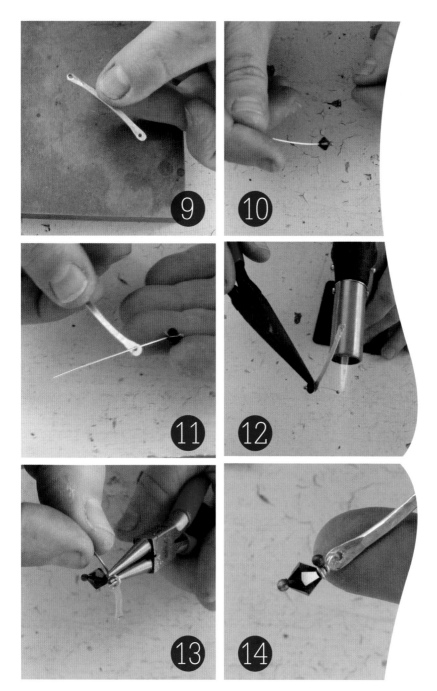

9. Remember to drill a hole in both ends.

10. Make a headpin by drawing a bead on one end of a 4" (10cm) piece of 22-gauge wire. Thread a bead onto it.

11. Thread the headpin through the bottom hole on one metal piece.

12. Draw a bead on the other end of the wire, using a torch. (See page 31.)

13. With the metal strip slid down and out of the way, create a loop at the base of the bead using round-nose pliers.

14. Slide the metal strip back up and into the loop you made. Wrap the excess wire around itself until all the wire is used up. Repeat steps 10 through 14 for the second wire.

Tip

There are numerous ways to create variations on this project. You could leave the hole and crystal dangle off of the bottom, or you could use a forming block (see page 89) to create a wavy pattern along the length of the chased wire as just a couple of ideas.

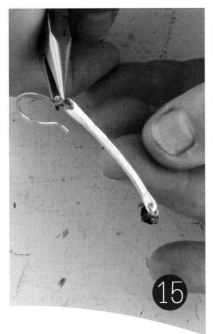

15. Make a pair of French ear wires from the 20-gauge sterling silver wire. (See page 33.) Thread one through the top end of each metal piece and crimp the loop closed.

16. Dip the pieces in liver of sulfur.

17. Polish the pieces with steel wool.

punched circle earrings

These earrings build on your forging/chasing and texturizing skills. In addition, they help
you learn to use a disc cutter more precisely. The inspiration came from a sterling silver
necklace I made for a friend who doesn't often wear jewelry. She liked the texture and
minimal design of the disc when strung onto a simple chain. This design can be used for
earrings as I show here, but also as a pendant or even as a bracelet focal. Make a dozen
of these punched circles and join them together for a statement necklace.

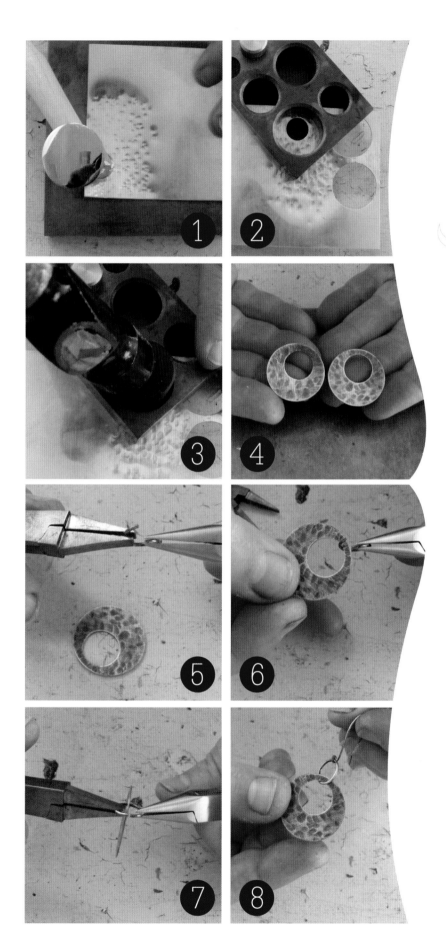

Tools

steel bench block

ball-peen hammer

disc cutter

dead-blow hammer

wire cutters

round-nose pliers

flat-nose pliers

Materials

20-gauge wire, sterling silver

22-gauge sheet metal, sterling silver

liver of sulfur

steel wool

1. Working on a steel block, texture the metal sheet with a ball-peen hammer. (Sterling silver or bronze is especially pretty.)

2. Using a disc cutter, punch a small hole in the sheet. Then position the sheet under a larger hole so the first hole is off center a bit.

3. With the cutting die in the cutter, use a hammer to punch out the larger circle.

4. Repeat for the second disc so you are left with two completed circles. Patina the discs in liver of sulfur and polish with steel wool.

5. Using 20-gauge wire, create two to four jump rings (see page 32). Using two pairs of pliers, twist open the first ring.

6. Thread one of the punched circles onto the open ring.

7. Use two pliers to twist the ring shut, snuggling up the ends together so they meet nicely. If you would like the earrings to be more dangly, you can add a second jump ring.

8. Create a pair of French ear wires (see page 33) and thread one ring onto the hook of each wire.

dapped and domed earrings

Cutting exact circles from metal sheet is a cinch with a disc cutter. These earrings are
an example of both form and scale in metal jewelry design, while also allowing for some
whimsy in the use of two different texture hammers. The slight dome shape and long ear
wires keep them looking chic.

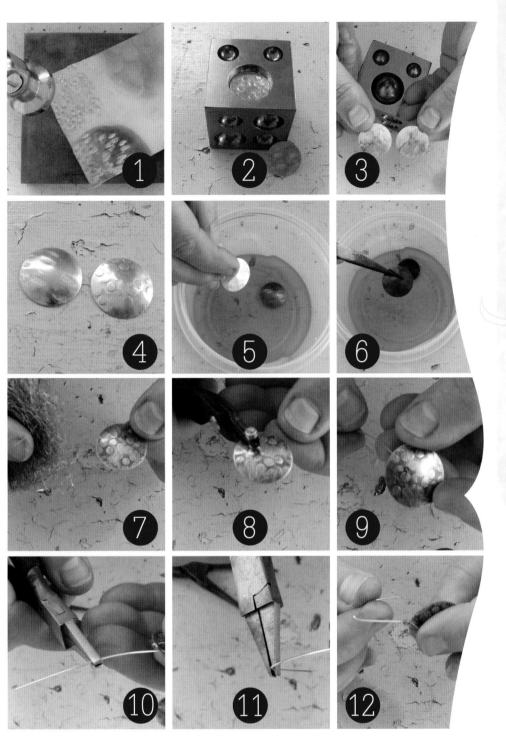

Tools

texturizing hammer(s)

steel bench block

disc cutter

hammer

dapping set

hole punch, $\frac{1}{16}$" (2mm) or drill

wire cutters

chain-nose pliers

file

Materials

20-gauge wire, sterling silver

22-gauge sheet metal, sterling silver

liver of sulfur

steel wool

1. To start this project, select your favorite texturing hammer. (Or be creative and use alternative tools and a regular hammer to create some texture.) Use your chosen hammer to apply texture over the surface of the metal sheet. Be sure to hammer on a steel bench block to get the best impression of the texture onto the metal. You can use a variety of textures if you like. Here I am using dots and stripes.

2. One at a time, cut two discs of the same size from the textured sheet using the disc cutter. Put one disc into the dapping block.

3. Use a dapping die and block to make dome shapes out of the discs.

4. My discs are nonmatching; I used two different textures for them, but you can make yours identical if you like.

5. Put the discs in a warm liver of sulfur solution.

6. Remove the discs when they are blackened using pliers that you don't mind getting oxidized.

7. Dry the discs and polish them with steel wool.

8. Punch a hole about $\frac{1}{8}$" (3mm) from the edge of each disc.

9. Thread a headpin made from 20-gauge wire through one of the holes.

10. At about $\frac{1}{4}$" (6mm) from the bead, bend the wire into a sharp U shape and crimp it slightly to the disc. About halfway down the remaining length of wire, begin a bend with chain-nose pliers.

11. Bend the wire into a V shape.

12. Using your fingers, make a slight curve to the end of the wire. File the ends of the ear wire so they are smooth.

forged and formed hoop earrings

When I worked at a newspaper in the 1990s, I always wore my gold hoops to work. They were professional and classic. Hoops have made a comeback in fashion, particularly giant round ones. Now that I'm living an artist's life, I still love my hoops, but I desire a hand-hammered and more spontaneous expression to them.

Tools

    wire cutters

    file

    ball-peen hammer

    torch

    firebrick or annealing pan

    copper tongs

    center punch

    hole punch, 1/16" (2mm) or drill

    bracelet mandrel

    dead-blow hammer

    flat-nose pliers

    round-nose pliers

    small mandrel

    needle-nose or chain-nose pliers

Materials

    16-gauge wire, sterling silver

    20-gauge wire, sterling silver

    22-gauge wire, bronze

    pickle

    liver of sulfur

1. Cut two 4" (10cm) pieces of 16-gauge wire and file the ends of each wire flat. Beginning with one piece, forge the entire length of the wire on both sides.

2. Add texture to the piece with a ball-peen hammer. Use the hammer to flatten the ends even more to paddle them. Anneal the sterling silver wire using a torch until the wire is dull red.

3. Quench the wire in water.

4. Dip the wire in pickling solution to remove fire-scale using copper tongs.

5. Use a file to nicely round the paddled ends . Center-punch for a hole at each end of the wire, centering it in the paddle portion.

6. Drill holes at the center-punched marks.

7. Use a bracelet mandrel or similar large round object to shape the wire into a hoop.

8. Use a hammer to work harden the shape.

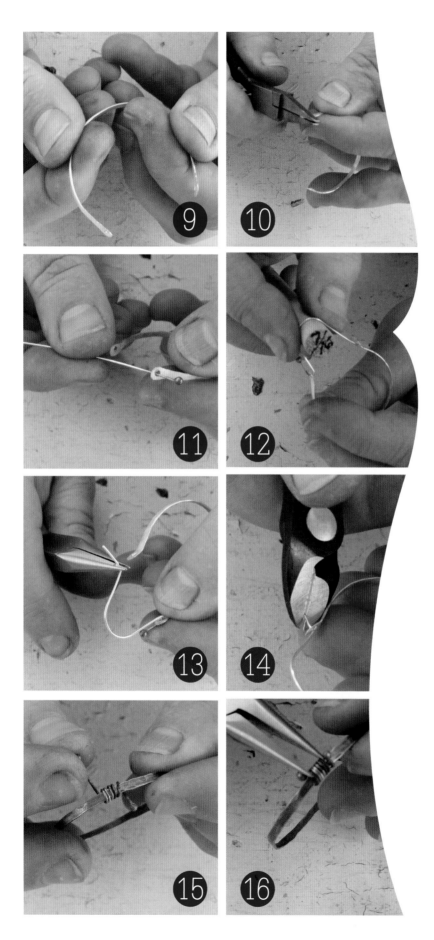

9. Complete any further shaping that might be needed with your hands.

10. Using flat-nose pliers, bend each end out a bit to form a horseshoe shape.

11. Feed a headpin made from 20-gauge wire through one of the holes.

12. Using round-nose pliers, create a small U about ¼" (6mm) from the ball head to act as a hook. Shape the wire into a U over a small mandrel.

13. Use needle-nose or chain-nose pliers to bend the end of the wire so it will thread easily through the hole on the other side of the hoop.

14. Hook the wire through the hole, and trim the excess wire to leave about a ⅛" (3mm) tail. File the end of the wire.

15. Repeat steps 7 through 14 for the other earring, and patina the earrings in liver of sulfur. Create a metal fiber from 22-gauge wire that is about 3" (8cm) and begin wrapping the wire around the center of the hoop.

16. Adjust the wrapped wire with pliers as needed. Repeat the metal-fiber wrap with a second wire for the other earring.

watch & learn

www.createmixedmedia.com/
makingmetaljewelry

EAR CUFF
Use the QR code here to see a video of Jen showing you how to
make this project.

simple cross earrings

I made a cross necklace for my mother-in-law right after she returned from a pilgrimage with her church to Jerusalem and Turkey. She was showing me pictures of the landscape, and I was enamored by the rough-hewn walls and ancient textures. If I had been on the trip, my hands would have touched and felt every piece of architecture. The textures shown in her photos and the symbolism of her trip inspired me to create this design.

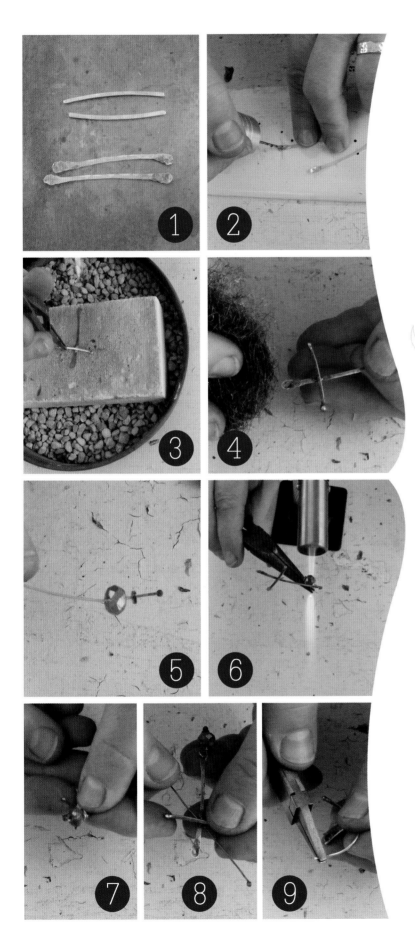

Tools

wire cutters

ball-peen hammer

torch

flat-nose pliers

center punch

hole punch, 1/16" (2mm) or drill

Solderite board

titanium pick tweezers

needle-nose pliers

round-nose pliers

file

Materials

18-gauge wire, sterling silver

20-gauge wire, sterling silver

22-gauge wire, bronze

pickle

silver solder paste

liver of sulfur

steel wool

crystal beads

heishi spacer beads

1. Cut two 2" (5cm) pieces of 20-gauge wire. Also cut two 2" (5cm) pieces of 18-gauge wire. Forge all four pieces of wire, and make paddle ends on the two 18-gauge pieces.

2. Draw a bead on both ends of the remaining two wires. Quench and pickle. Center-punch both paddled ends of the longer pieces and then drill holes at each divot.

3. Apply a tiny bit of paste solder to one long piece, about one-third of the way from one end. Use tweezers to hold one short piece over the long piece and heat with a propane torch to melt the paste solder and join the pieces together.

4. Repeat for the other cross. Pickle, patina (liver of sulphur) and polish the crosses.

5. Thread a heishi spacer (or tiny washer) and a crystal onto a 22-gauge head pin.

6. Thread the wire through the bottom hole on one cross. Using the torch and using needle-nose pliers to hold the crystal as far from the flame as possible, draw a bead on the other end of the headpin.

7. About 1/4" (6mm) from the crystal, start a loop in the wire using round-nose pliers. Slide the bottom of one cross into the loop and wrap the remaining wire around the base of the loop, until you get to the end of the headpin where the second bead was drawn.

8. Take a metal fiber and cross-wrap it at the center of the cross. Wrap the wire a couple of times in each direction.

9. Repeat steps 3 through 8 for the other cross. Attach a French ear wire (see page 33) to the top hole of each cross to finish.

metal bracelets and rings

Are you feeling warmed up yet? It's time to create some rings and bracelets. Some of my favorite projects are found in this chapter. (Shushhhhh . . . don't tell anyone because a momma is never supposed to pick favorites, but I'm really partial to my Fork Bracelet. It's exhilarating to take a utilitarian object and re-purpose it into something unexpected.) Some of the techniques you'll practice in this chapter include forging and texturizing, forming and bending, wire wrapping, riveting and cold enamel.

free-form forged bangles

I've always loved the look of a wrist full of bangles, but I've never been able to find ones that fit me properly. That was until I started making forged free-form bangles with open ends, which provide more flexibility when slipping them over the hands. You can change the look of these metal bangles depending on where you decide to end the circle. You can stop the ends so they fit just beyond the wrist bones with a little space between or overlap them for a free-form look. If you want more structure, you can also join the ends together and cold connect them with rivets or eyelets.

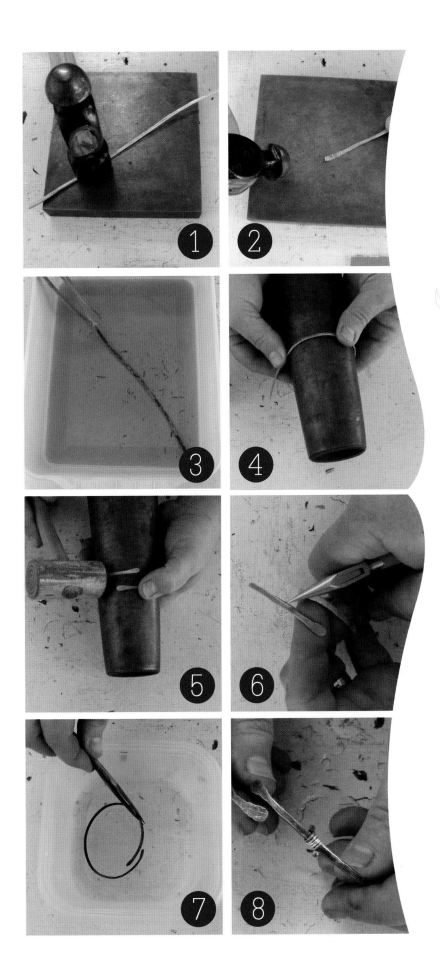

Tools

heavy-duty flush cutters

ball-peen hammer

steel bench block

file

torch

firebrick or annealing pan

copper tongs

bracelet mandrel

dead-blow hammer

flat-nose pliers

wire cutters

Materials

12-gauge wire, bronze

20-gauge wire, sterling silver

Jax Brown patina

pickle

steel wool

1. Cut a length of 12-gauge bronze wire to 7" or 8" (18cm or 20cm) and forge the entire length of the wire.

2. Hammer paddles on each end as well.

3. File any rough burrs off the paddles. Anneal the entire wire to a cherry red and let it cool slightly before quenching in water. Immerse the wire into nickel pickle using copper tongs.

4. Use your hands to form the wire around a bracelet mandrel so the ends cross a bit—rather like a coil.

5. Work harden the wire on the mandrel with a hammer.

6. Bend the ends of the bracelet inward just slightly using flat-nose pliers.

7. Immerse the bracelet into some Jax blackening solution.

8. Blot off the solution, then polish the bracelet with steel wool. Wrap a contrasting metal fiber around the bracelet at one end.

organic wire-wrapped bracelet

This project is similar to my organic shawl pin in that the technique is taking a long piece of wire and hand manipulating it into form. The most important part about this technique is to use your fingers and keep your dominant hand that's doing the wrapping loose so the beads and links have a light, airy look when finished. The addition of the two large-hole, pavé crystal beads and organza fabric provides a pop of color, but this project is gorgeous when designed with wire alone, particularly mixed metals.

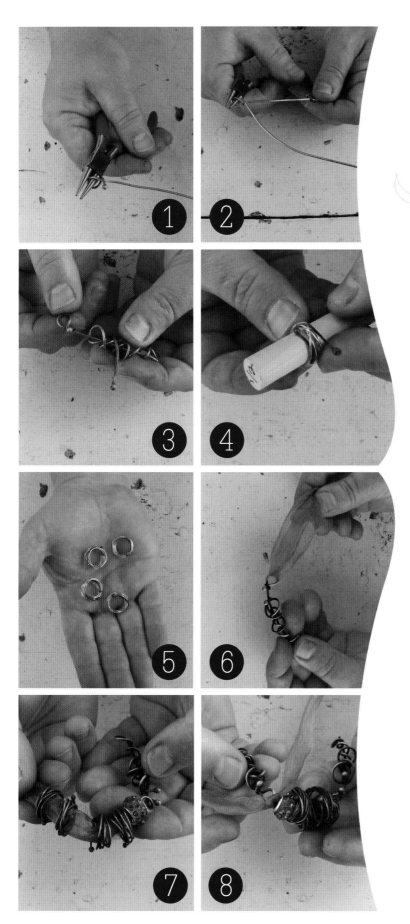

Tools

wire cutters

torch

round-nose pliers

scissors

ball-peen hammer

steel bench block

Materials

16-gauge wire, bronze

18-gauge wire, bronze

20-gauge wire, bronze

organza ribbon

large-hole crystal beads, 2

½" (13mm) dowel or mandrel

steel wool

1. Cut two 12" (30cm) pieces of 16-gauge wire. Draw beads on both ends of both wires using MAPP gas. Heat patina the entire length of the wire. Quench and polish a bit. Take one wire and make a loop on one end using round-nose pliers.

2. Make a second loop about 2" (5cm) from the first loop.

3. Holding onto the last loop with one hand, use your other hand to loosely wrap the remaining wire around the length of the loop.

4. Repeat for the other wire to make a second organic link. Patina again and polish the links. Cut five 12" (30cm) pieces of 20-gauge wire and draw a bead on the end of each wire. Wrap each wire in a messy coil around a dowel.

5. Four complete coils will be used for the bracelet; the fifth will be used for the toggle clasp.

6. Cut an 8" (20cm) length of organza ribbon. Thread it through one of the messy links and fold in half.

7. Thread a large-holed bead onto the ribbon. Then thread on four coiled pieces.

8. Thread on the second large-holed bead. Tie the remaining ribbon ends to one end of the second messy link, leaving a little slack in the ribbon.

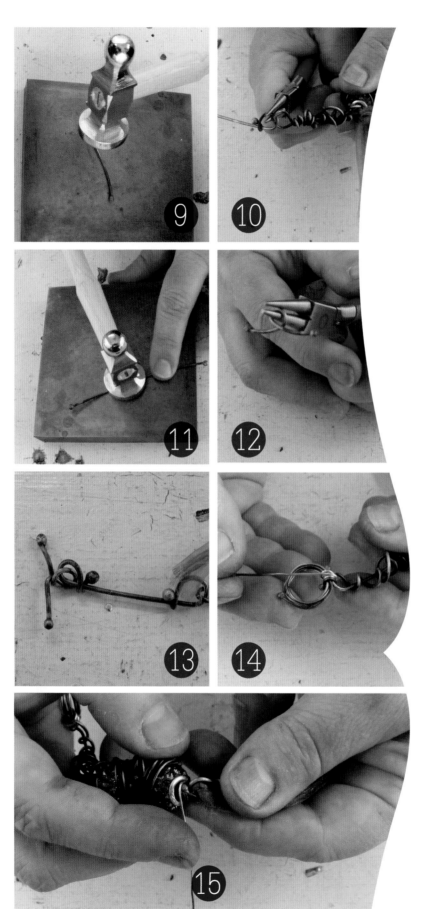

9. Cut a 4" (10cm) length of 18-gauge wire, draw a bead on each end and then forge the metal fiber a bit.

10. Thread this fiber through one of the end links and make a loop to connect it.

11. Cut a 2" (5cm) length of 18-gauge wire and draw a bead on each end. Forge the metal fiber a bit to work harden it.

12. Fold it into a U shape and cross the wires, creating a loop.

13. Thread the toggle onto the other end link and twist the wire to cinch it closed.

14. Cut a 4" (10cm) length of 18-gauge wire and draw a bead on each end. Use this to wrap the remaining coil to the other end of the bracelet.

15. Wrap a final metal fiber around the section where the ribbon tails are to get them pointed nicely in the same direction.

alternative metal

WIRE-WRAPPED BANGLE

This type of bracelet doesn't have to include ribbons and fibers.
The organic wrapping looks equally great on an all-metal version.

For more ideas, check out www.createmixedmedia.com/
makingmetaljewelry

upcycled cuff with metal focal

Like many mixed-media artists, I'm always searching for ways to repurpose interesting materials into new work. Leather belts bought for a few dollars at secondhand stores make a lovely bracelet substrate for an organic metal focal element and gorgeous fibers. If the belt you purchase has a slick coating to it, immerse the belt in water to soften the leather and then take a palm sander to it. I have an industrial belt sander from my father-in-law that makes quick work of dulling down shiny finishes.

Tools

shears or scissors

jeweler's saw

dead-blow hammer

file

doming set

ball-peen hammer

round-nose pliers

center punch

hole punch, 1/16" (2mm) or drill

steel bench block

tapestry needle

flat-nose pliers

Materials

22-gauge metal sheet, etched brass

22-gauge wire, bronze

leather belt

fibers

decorative nail head rivet

Jax Brown patina

steel wool

1. Measure a length of leather from a belt that will fit around your wrist, minus about 1" (3cm).

2. Cut the leather with shears or scissors.

3. Sand the smooth finish off the belt if there is one.

4. Using shears or a jeweler's saw, cut an organic circle shape from a piece of etched metal, about the size of a half-dollar.

5. File the edges smooth and patina the circle with Jax Brown. Then polish with steel wool. Using a large dome in the dapping block, dap the circle. Don't worry about making a perfect dome—the shape should be irregular.

6. Using round-nose pliers, randomly roll the edge of the circle back at about three spots.

7. Center-punch the center of the metal circle. Drill a hole at the divot made by the center punch.

8. Using the circle's hole as a guide, mark a hole in the leather where the circle will be attached.

9. Drill a hole in the leather where marked.

10. Mark for two holes on the opposite end of the leather, about ½" (13mm) in from the edges and end.

11. Drill the two holes.

12. Insert the rivet through the circle and the leather from the front to the back.

13. Turn the piece over and begin setting the rivet on the back by tapping around the perimeter of the wire with a ball-peen hammer.

14. Hammer it gently on the front as well.

15. Using a tapestry needle or a scrap of wire, push the fiber through the remaining holes from the front to the back.

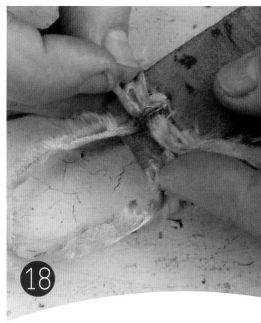

16. Leave a large loop to act as the clasp.

17. Make certain the loop is large enough to fit around the metal circle and still fit your wrist. Tie the tails on the back. Tie a knot. Bring the tails around to the front again and tie in a knot. Trim the excess fiber if necessary.

18. Add any final embellishment if you like, such as this metal fiber I'm adding here.

fork bracelet

Jewelry made from repurposed spoons has been popular for a long time, but I started thinking that I rarely see pieces made from other types of cutlery. This led me to experiment with forks. I made a series of rings, necklaces and bracelets. This piece is my favorite from that design series. I like the way the tines are formed inward with long round-nose pliers to create a holder for the wire pieces, a technique that I believe lends a sculptural quality to the bracelet.

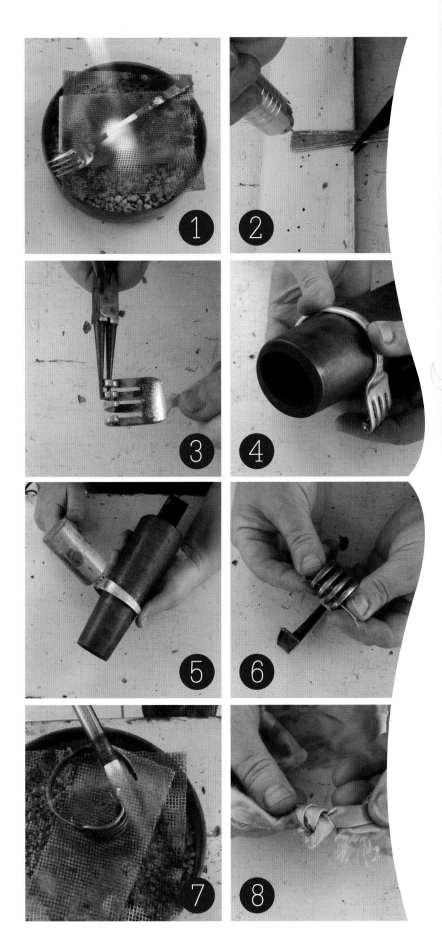

1. Anneal a fork using MAPP gas.

2. Quench the fork and then pickle. Use the center punch to mark for a hole at the end of the fork's handle. Holding the fork with pliers, drill a hole at the center-punched mark.

3. Using long round-nose pliers, curl the tines of the fork inward.

4. Begin shaping the fork around a bracelet mandrel with your hands.

5. Fine-tune the shape using a hammer.

6. Patina the fork and polish with steel wool. (Note: Unless you are certain of the type of metal your fork is, you may need to try both kinds of patina [JAX and liver of sulfur] to get results.) Cut two 2½" (6mm) pieces of 14-gauge wire. Draw a bead on one end of each and work harden each wire a bit. Thread the wires through the tines.

7. Set the fork so the blunt ends of the wires face up on the firing screen and draw a bead on the blunt ends.

8. Quench the bracelet. If the wires feel like they might fall out, tighten the tines as needed. Begin the flower. Start with a 24" (61cm) strip of frayed ribbon or fabric and fold it in half. Tie a knot on the end with the tails, creating one large loop.

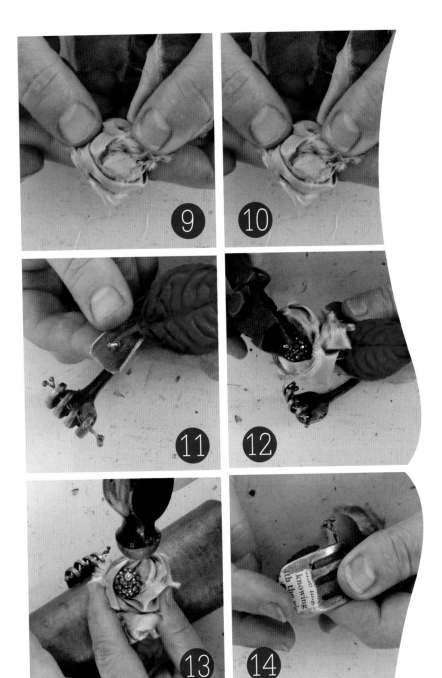

9. Begin the center of the flower by rolling up the folded ribbon at the knot end.

10. Thread a needle and begin using it to tack the ribbon together at the back/bottom as you roll up the flower.

11. Continue until the ribbon is completely rolled. Tie off the thread. Thread a micro bolt through the handle of the fork from the inside to the outside. Twist a silk leaf around the bolt.

12. Push the bolt through the rose, then thread on the bead. Tighten the nut down to secure everything and then trim off the excess length of the bolt.

13. Splay the end of the bolt with a hammer, working on a bracelet mandrel.

14. Finally, if you like, adhere a word to the fork using gel medium or varnish.

Tip

Because forks are a "found object" metal, it's not always possible to know what they are made of. Sterling silver forks are the easiest to work with, but the hardest to find these days. Silver-plated are easy to find, but the finish often burns and bubbles as you torch it. This project is one of experimentation, and results can be different depending on the types of metal used.

watch & learn

TASSLE
Use the QR code here to see a video of Jen showing you how to make this project.

www.createmixedmedia.com/
makingmetaljewelry

forged ring

Forging is so much fun to do that I keep dreaming up new projects where I can hammer and anneal heavy-gauge wire into something fabulous. These little rings came about because I wanted a new spin on the traditional band ring. Rather than soldering the ends together, I decided to work harden the ends so they remain slightly flexible. A bit of soldering does come into play, however, with some cute little decorative balls that are added to the ends of the band and then forged flat.

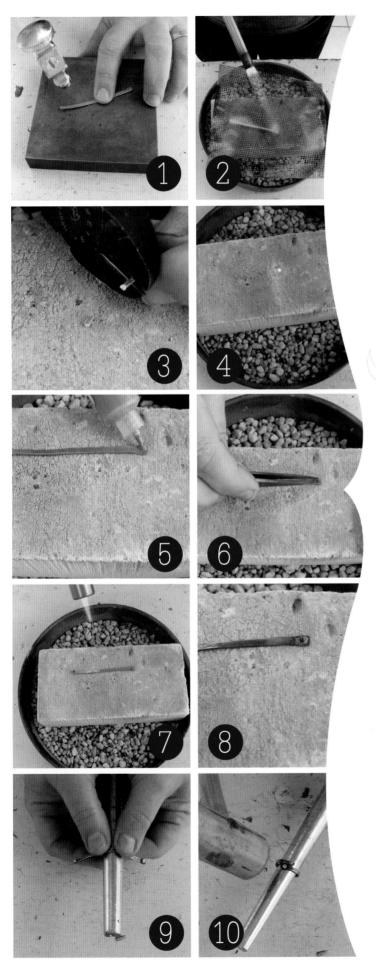

Tools

heavy-duty flush cutters

file

ball-peen hammer

steel bench block

torch with MAPP gas

annealing pan

wire cutters

tweezers

butane torch

Solderite board

ring mandrel

dead-blow hammer

Materials

12-gauge wire, bronze

20-gauge wire, sterling silver

sterling silver solder paste

Jax Brown patina

pickle

steel wool

1. Trim a piece of 12-gauge bronze wire to about 1" (3cm) larger than your ring size. File the ends of the wire. Forge the wire with a hammer and also paddle the ends of the wire. (See page 17.) Switch to a smaller ball-peen hammer to create a bit of texture over the strip.

2. Anneal the wire until it gets cherry red.

3. Cut off two little "chips" of sterling wire (20-gauge).

4. Heat the chips with the torch until they form little glowing balls and then let it cool.

5. Apply a bit of paste solder to the center of the paddles on each end of the strip.

6. Using tweezers, set the silver balls onto the solder.

7. Use a butane torch with a low flame to heat and melt the silver paste solder.

8. Quench the band. Use a ball-peen hammer to flatten the little balls a bit. Pickle the band to remove the firescale, patina, and then polish with steel wool.

9. Form the ring around a ring mandrel.

10. Use a hammer to work harden the band around the mandrel.

cold enamel ring

I use a jeweler's grade, two-part epoxy resin that's nontoxic when cured in a lot of my mixed-media work. It can be used to encase objects in bezels, as a sealant, as an adhesive and even—as you see here—to re-create the look of enameling. Because it's jeweler's-grade, my work will last forever. Color is an important consideration in my aesthetic, so I'm always looking for ways to incorporate it into my metalwork. I think this little technique easily gets the job done.

Tools

shears

file

dapping set

ball-peen hammer

annealing pan with vermiculite

butane torch

disposable paintbrush

wire cutters

metal leaf stamp

steel bench block

hole punch, 1/16" (2mm) or drill

ring mandrel

dead-blow hammer

flat-nose pliers

Materials

22-gauge metal sheet, copper

20-gauge wire, sterling silver

paper towels

assorted oil pastels

epoxy resin (ICE)

sterling silver solder paste

Jax Brown patina

pickle

steel wool

micro bolt and nut

crystal rondelle

1. Cut an organic lopsided circle from 22-gauge copper sheet using shears.

2. File the edges smooth. Place the circular shape in the largest dapping dome and shape it with the die and hammer. Move down in size until you have the flower shape you are happy with.

3. Place the flower shape in vermiculite and heat it a bit with a butane torch. Begin adding color with an oil pastel, spreading the color a bit as it melts.

4. Alternate between heating areas and coloring on them. Add more colors.

5. Continue until you have a nice pool of assorted colors. Don't heat the copper too much or you'll burn up the pastel.

6. Wad up a wet paper towel and create a wreath shape to set the flower in so it rests upright.

7. Mix up a tiny amount of resin according to manufacturer's directions. I prefer using ICE Resin because you can buy it as a plunger and disperse very small amounts at a time. Squeeze out a small bit into a disposable cup and mix it according to the package directions.

8. Use a disposable paintbrush to paint the resin over the surface of the flower.

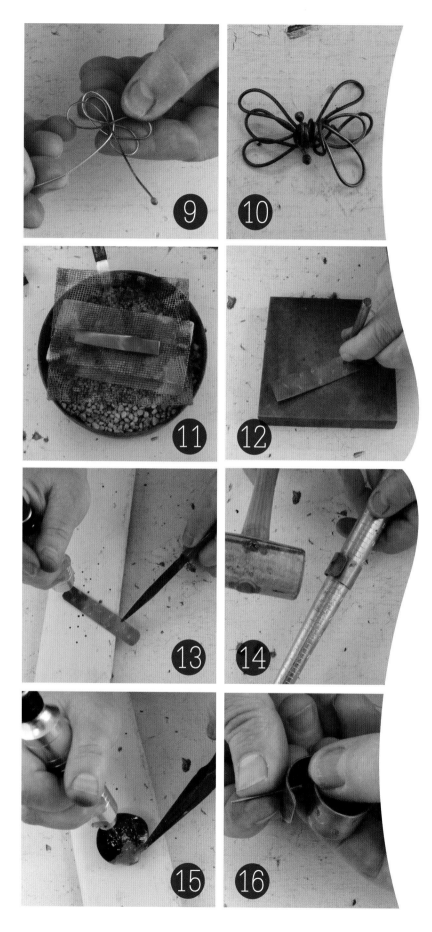

9. Set the resin-filled flower aside to cure (about 8 hours). Cut a 12" (30cm) piece of 20-gauge bronze wire, draw a bead at each end and heat patina. Begin free-form shaping the wire into a loopy shape that resembles a gift bow.

10. Wrap the ends of the wire loosely around the center.

11. Cut a piece of 22-gauge copper sheet to ½" x 3" (13mm x 8cm). Anneal the metal using a torch.

12. Quench and add texture with metal stamps. Here I am using a leaf design.

13. Snip the corners and round them with a file. Drill a hole ½" (13mm) from one end and centered in the width of the strip.

14. Patina the piece and polish. Form the strip around a ring mandrel, overlapping the ends a bit to make the ring adjustable. The end with the hole should be on the outside.

15. Drill a hole in the center of the cured flower.

16. To assemble the ring, thread the bolt from the inside of the ring out.

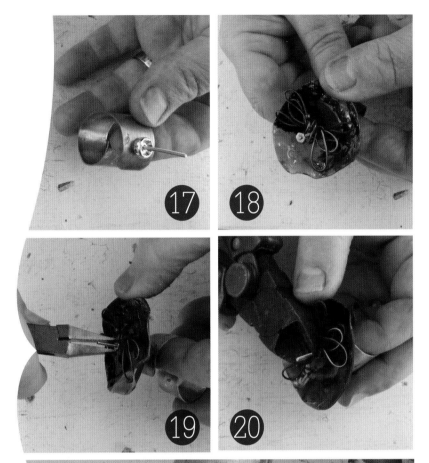

17. Holding the bolt head against the ring shank with your finger or thumb, thread on a crystal rondelle.

18. Thread on the enameled flower, then the loopy wire shape (create a hole through it using the bolt), then a nut.

19. Tighten the nut down with pliers.

20. Snip off the excess bolt with wire cutters.

21. Place the ring back on the ring mandrel to reshape a bit if needed.

spinner ring

One of the most innovative techniques I've learned is how to add kinetic movement to jewelry. This spinner ring is a perfect example of how to take a simple ring and make it more interesting with the addition of moving parts. You can't help but find yourself spinning the focal bead in this ring whenever you wear it. It's particularly fun to wear on boring meeting days at work.

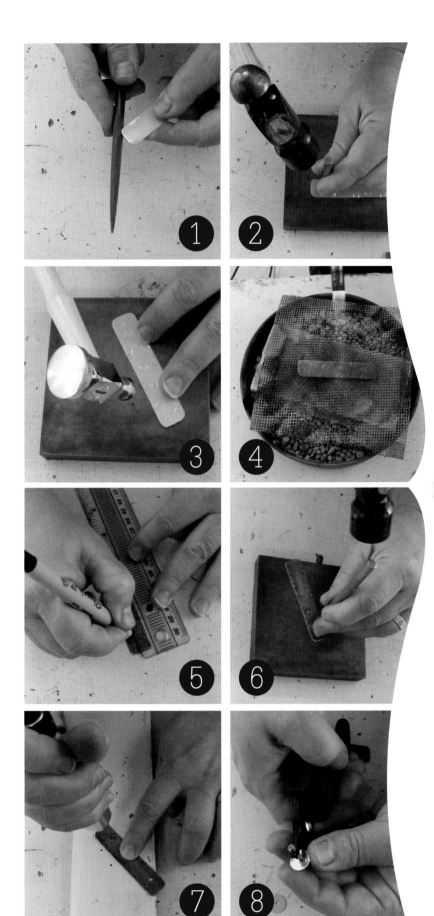

Tools

shears

file

dead-blow hammer

steel bench block

circle pattern metal stamp

ball-peen hammer

torch

annealing pan

center punch

hole punch, ⅟₁₆" (2mm) or drill

disc cutter

dapping set

ring mandrel

flat-nose pliers

heavy-duty flush cutters

Materials

22-gauge sheet metal, sterling silver

permanent marker

large crystal bead

pickle

liver of sulfur

long micro bolt and nut

heishi spacer beads

steel wool

1. Using shears, cut a piece of metal sheet to ½" x 4" (13mm x 10cm) and use a file to round the corners and smooth the edges.

2. Add texture to the metal with a hammer and one or more metal stamps.

3. Deckle the edges of the metal with a ball-peen hammer.

4. Anneal the metal.

5. Pickle, patina and polish the piece. Measure down ½" (13mm) from each edge and make a mark at the center of the width of the strip using a permanent marker. (See Tip on page 80 for additional info.)

6. Center-punch the marks lightly with a hammer and punch. (Do not use a spring-loaded punch or you might go through the metal.)

7. Drill holes at the marks.

8. Cut out two ½" (13mm) discs from the metal sheet and punch a ⅟₁₆" (2mm) hole in the center of each.

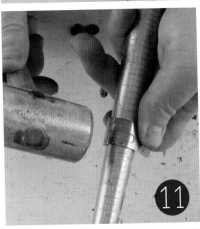

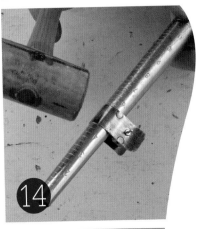

Tip

The bead you select for this project will have a large impact on the finished size of the ring, as will the position of the drilled holes in the metal strip. After you have shaped the ring into a U, check for size by holding the bead you want to use between the strips and against your finger to make certain where to drill the holes and also whether the bead will make the ring too big or too small.

9. To create bead caps, dap each disc into a dome shape. Start with a larger dap and then progress to a smaller shape.

10. Patina the caps in liver of sulfur and polish with steel wool. Form the metal strip around a ring mandrel.

11. Shape the piece over the mandrel using a hammer. Check the alignment as you work to make sure the holes are aligned nicely.

12. Use flat-nose pliers to gently bend the ends back a bit.

13. Thread a micro bolt through a heshi bead, then through one side of the ring from the outside to the inside. On the inside, thread the bolt through one bead cap, then the large bead, the other bead cap and the other side of the ring.

14. Thread the nut onto the bolt. Push the ring back on the ring mandrel and reshape it, if needed, with a hammer.

15. Trim the excess bolt with flush cutters and file it.

alternative metal

SPINNER PENDANT VARIATION

For this design, instead of creating a ring, I fashioned the element as a pendant. The spinning crystals are just as much fun to play with as the bead on the ring. Another switch up: I secured the axis for the bead by drawing a bead on the ends of a wire instead of using a micro nut and bolt.

For more ideas, check out www.createmixedmedia.com/makingmetaljewelry

metal pendants and necklaces

Necklaces offer a plethora of different design options. I think I shall never grow tired of making mixed-media jewelry because there are hundreds of looks I can get out of the techniques featured in this final chapter of the book. Just like the projects created thus far, these pendants and necklaces are made by hand from beginning to end. You'll get much more comfortable with your torch and soldering in this section when you learn to make your own bezels; you'll be introduced to the wonders of fold-forming; and you'll get much more practice with metal stamping and chain making.

charm-holder necklace

When I was a teenager, my mother bought me a charm holder for my fifteenth birthday. Now that I've learned to make jewelry, I love to re-create the U-shaped charm holder from wire. Drawing a bead on each end of the wire that threads through the U shape keeps it secure. I've made charms from bead dangles, found objects and even these colorful lampwork beads. For this project, the glass bird charm looks so cute sitting in her dapped and domed metal nest.

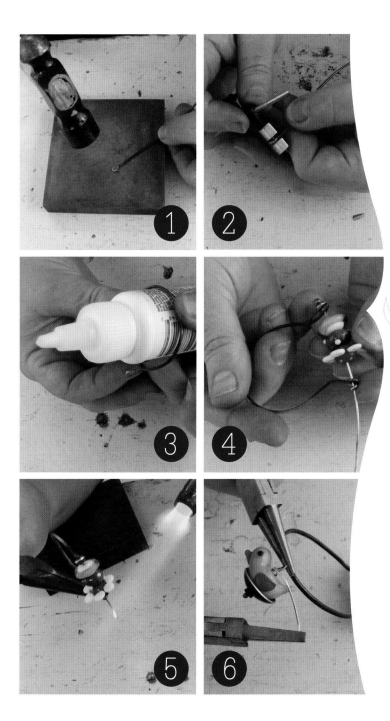

Tools

wire cutters

torch

dead-blow hammer

steel bench block

ball-peen hammer

two-hole screw punch

large mandrel such as
a glue bottle

flat-nose pliers

disc cutter

dapping set

1/16" (2mm) or drill

round-nose pliers

scissors

Materials

14-gauge wire,
bronze

18-gauge wire,
sterling silver

20-gauge wire,
sterling silver

Jax Brown patina

steel wool

crystals

heishi spacer beads

1/2" (13m) dapped
dome disc, any metal

silk ribbon

bronze garter clips

lampwork beads

bronze jump rings

1. Cut a 6" (15cm) length of 14-gauge wire. Draw a bead on each end. Forge the entire length of the wire and also flatten the beads on the ends of the wire.

2. Add texture using a ball-peen hammer. Punch a hole in the center of each flattened bead using a two-hole screw punch.

3. Using a glue bottle as a mandrel, form the wire into a U shape.

4. Use flat-nose pliers to bend the ends back just a bit. Patina in JAX and polish. Cut a 2½" (6cm) piece of 18- or 20-gauge sterling silver wire and draw a bead on one end. Thread the wire through a spacer bead and then through the charm holder. Then, thread on a series of lampwork beads. Thread the wire through the other side of the charm holder.

5. Thread a second spacer bead onto the wire, then trim the wire to leave about a ⅝" (16mm) tail. Draw a bead on that end of the wire, being careful to not overheat the glass beads.

6. To create the focal-point nest dangle, drill a hole in the center of the dome disc. Thread a headpin onto a spacer bead, then thread on the nest and a glass bird bead. Begin a loop using round-nose pliers. Thread the loop over the charm holder and finish wrapping the wire around the base of the loop.

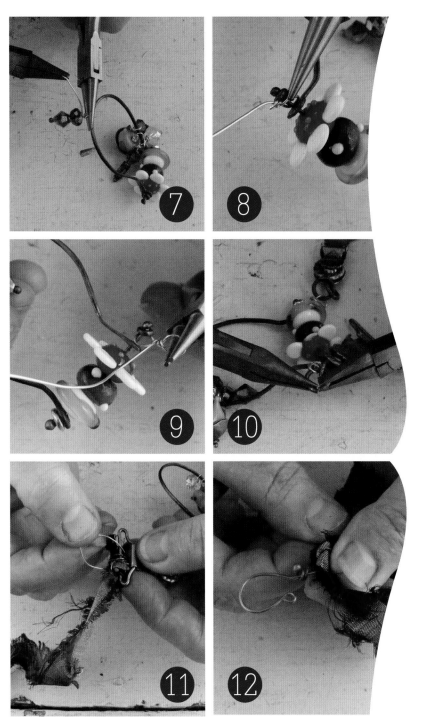

7. Create several more charm dangles with crystal beads and add those to the charm holder.

8. Cut two 4" (10cm) pieces of 20-gauge wire. With one piece, wrap the wire around the fiber going through the holder, between the wire bead and the spacer bead. Crimp the tail around the base of the loop.

9. Create a second, larger loop above the wrap using round-nose pliers.

10. Attach garter clips (or found objects of your choice) to the wire-wrapped hangers on the holder using a couple of jump rings.

11. Cut two 9" (23cm) pieces of silk ribbon and tie one onto each garter clip. Wrap a metal fiber around the knotted portion of the ribbon to reinforce the ribbon onto the clips.

12. Create a hook clasp and tie the ribbon onto each half of the clasp.

watch & learn

www.createmixedmedia.com/
makingmetaljewelry

CHARM EXCHANGE
Use the QR code here to see a video of Jen showing you how to make this project.

fold-formed pendant
with soldered chain

This project is an entry point into the fascinating world of metal fold-forming, where you literally anneal and fold metal as if you were making origami shapes. From this simple starting point, you can learn to shape and form metal into wondrous three-dimensional forms. All it takes is learning a few more techniques and spending some playtime in your studio. Fold-forming, in my humble opinion, is one of the best ways to learn the properties of metal and how it changes when work hardened and annealed over and over again.

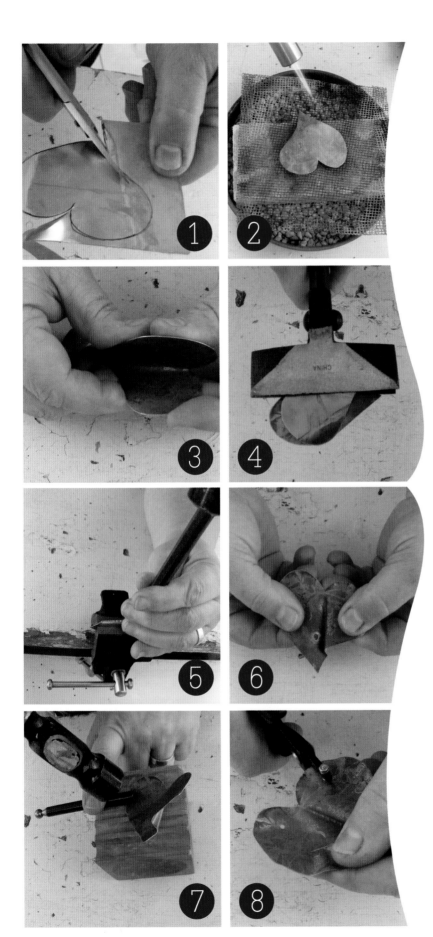

Tools

shears or jeweler's saw

file

butane torch

annealing pan

flat-nose pliers

vice

chisel

dead-blow hammer

doming mandrels

dapping block

hole punch, 1/16" (2mm) or drill

wire cutters

large round mandrel

Solderite board

round-nose pliers

Materials

24-gauge metal sheet, etched brass

16-gauge wire, bronze

22-gauge wire, bronze

paste solder

liver of sulphur

steel wool

1. Draw an asymmetrical heart onto the etched metal. Cut out the shape with shears.

2. File the edges to smooth. Anneal the heart shape.

3. Begin folding the shape with your hands. It can be folded in any spot.

4. Crimp the fold either with pliers or by pressing it in a vice.

5. With the folded edge raised a bit, use a chisel and a hammer to create a series of indentations along the fold.

6. Unfold the heart. (If it is too hard to unfold, anneal it again.)

7. Create flutes by hammering a die or mandrel into the flute side of a dapping block. Continue around the perimeter of the heart.

8. Punch or drill two holes for attaching the chain, at the lobes of the heart.

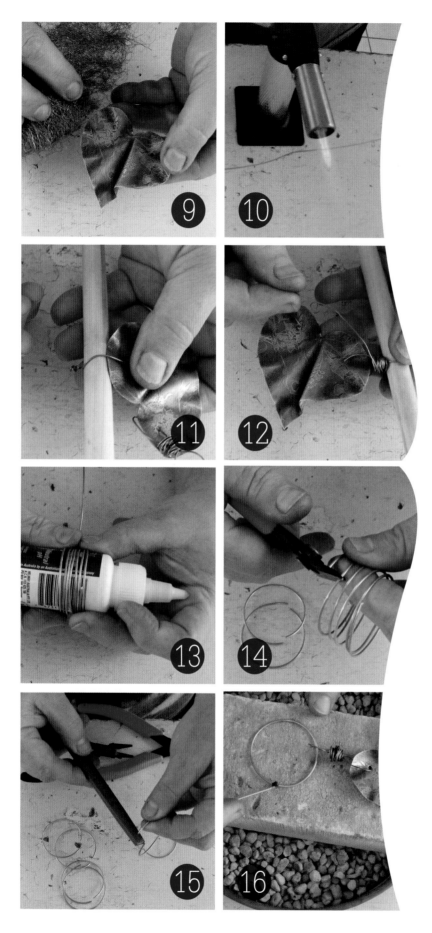

9. Patina the heart and then polish with steel wool.

10. Cut two 20" (51cm) pieces of 22-gauge wire and use a torch to patina them. (Alternatively, you could patina them in liver of sulfur.)

11. Thread one piece of wire through one of the holes in the heart. Using a 4" (10cm) tail, wrap the wire around a ½" (13mm) mandrel and twist the tail around the remaining wire.

12. Wrap the wire around the mandrel again and twist. Wrap the long length of wire numerous times around the twisted wire portion, creating a large, loopy wrap. Repeat steps 11 and 12 for the other hole in the heart.

13. Find a round object that is large enough to create "giant jump rings" and create a coil on it using 16-gauge wire. Here I am using a glue bottle. Coil the wire around the mandrel 8–12 times.

14. Snip the coil into 8–12 individual rings.

15. File the ends of the wires.

16. Snuggle the seam of the rings so they close tightly. Thread one ring onto one loop of the heart and set it on the Solderite board. Put a dab of paste solder onto the ring connection.

17. Begin heating the ring with the butane torch, heating the opposite end of the connection first. Solder the connection with the butane torch.

18. Add a second ring to the first ring using the same process. Note: To avoid accidentally melting the solder on your first ring, move the connection away from the second ring by rotating it.

19. Repeat for the remainder of the rings. Attach a shepherd's hook clasp (see page 35) to the end rings using a jump ring.

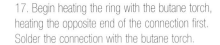

Tip

Using a piece of etched metal adds texture and depth to this heart. However, you can also use metal stamps or texturizing hammers and patina to achieve a similar look.

clay heart pendant

I'm drawn to the heart as a symbol because when I look at it, I'm instantly reminded of my family and their ever-present love and support. The addition of a hand-formed wire wing extends the symbolism because I like to surround myself with people whose positive energy makes me, and other people, feel like they can do anything when they're near. Because this piece is made from clay, it's really light and easy to wear.

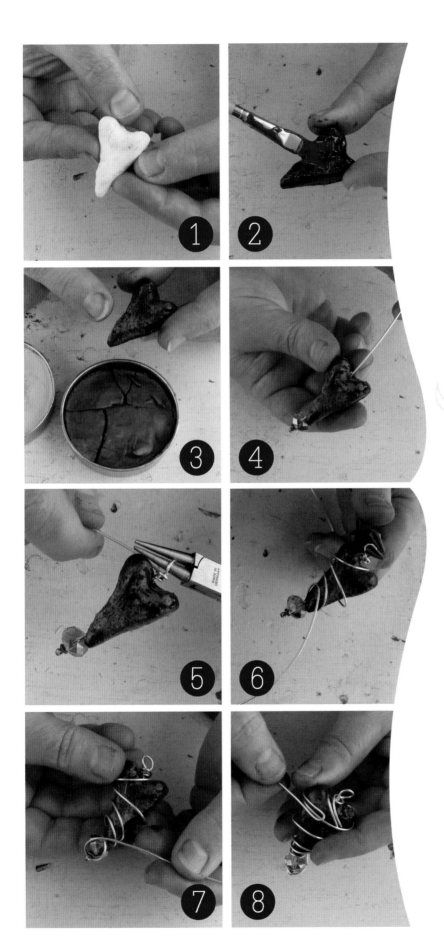

Tools	Materials
paintbrush	16-gauge wire, bronze
wire cutters	
torch	18-gauge wire, sterling silver
round-nose pliers	
ball-peen hammer	20-gauge wire, sterling silver
steel bench block	22-gauge sheet metal, sterling silver
shears	
annealing pan	paper clay
center punch	acrylic paint, black and red
hand-held hole punch	
	gilder's paste
dowel or mandrel, ⁷⁄₁₆" (11mm)	crystal bead
	pickle
file	liver of sulphur
	steel wool
	leather cording

1. Using your hands, mold the modeling clay into a heart shape.

2. When the heart is set, paint it with black acrylic paint. Then apply other colors, such as red, magenta or blue.

3. When the paint is dry, apply some gilder's paste to highlight various areas.

4. Cut a 36" (91cm) piece of 18-gauge sterling wire and draw a bead on one end. Thread a bead onto the wire and then push the wire through the center of the heart from the bottom to the top. (If you're using a clay that is more dense when it is cured—such as polymer or resin—you can drill a hole through the heart.)

5. Using round-nose pliers, make a wrapped loop at the top of the heart.

6. Now begin wrapping the wire randomly around the heart to create sort of a cage around it.

7. Catch the wire around the sterling bead at the bottom of the heart and begin winding it back up the heart.

8. When the wire is at the top of the heart, create a fold for the wire to point up.

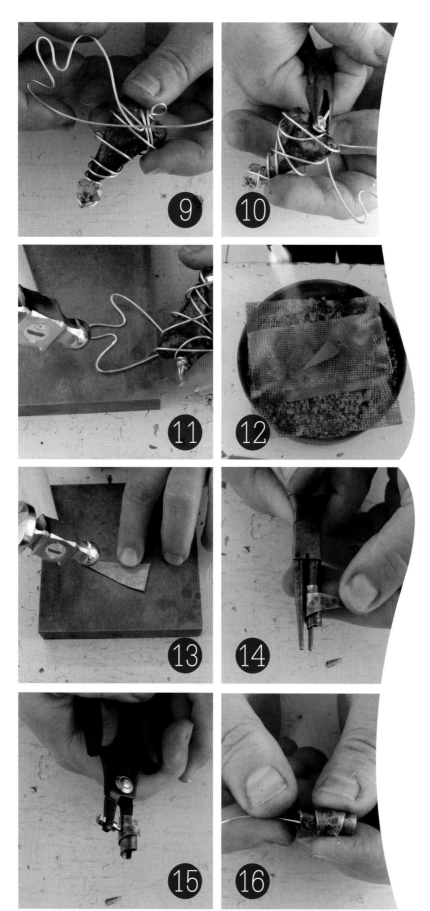

9. Free-form a wing shape from the wire. To secure the wing, thread the wire through the fold you made.

10. Wrap the wire a few times around the top loop of the heart, trim the excess wire and crimp it to secure.

11. Reshape the wing as needed, and then work harden it a bit with a ball-peen hammer to also give some texture to the wing.

12. To create the bail, cut a small triangle from the sterling silver sheet. Anneal the triangle, using a torch.

13. Quench and pickle the piece. Patina with liver of sulfur and polish. Add texture to the metal using a ball-peen hammer.

14. Roll the triangle up on a long pair of round-nose pliers.

15. When the bail is rolled, punch a hole in the center using a hand-held hole punch.

16. Cut a 3" (8cm) piece of 20-gauge wire and draw a bead on one end. Thread the headpin through the bail from the inside to the outside. You may need to make a slight curve in the wire to get it threaded through.

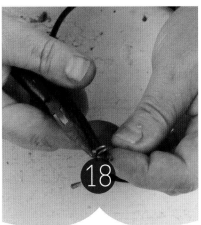

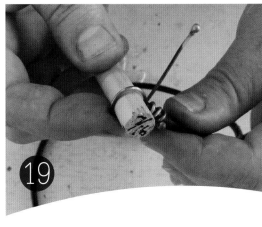

17. Thread the wire through the loop created at the top of the pendant and create a wrapped loop to connect the two pieces.

18. Cut a 16" (41cm) length of leather cord. Cut two 6" (15cm) pieces of 16-gauge bronze wire. Draw a bead on both ends of one wire and on one end of the other wire. Take the piece with beads on both ends and wrap one end of it around one end of the cord. Crimp it securely.

19. Wrap the wire around a 7/16" (11mm) dowel to make a large loop.

20. Wrap the rest of the wire around the leather again, then work harden the loop with a hammer.

21. Take the other wire and wrap the end with the bead around the other end of the leather and crimp it as you did the wire in step 18. Wrap the wire around the leather several times and then bend the wire straight up. Create a hook by forming the wire around the dowel. Trim the extra wire if necessary. Roll the tip of the wire back onto itself, using round-nose pliers.

22. Work harden the center of the hook.

stamped pendant with metal fiber chain

Because I was interested in exploring the art-making process from beginning to end, I challenged myself a couple of years ago to start producing work where I created every component. From the focal to the chain to the clasp, I made a series of pieces to reveal what I call the hand of the artist. It was from these experiments that I learned new chain-making skills. The image on the pendant is a photograph I took at an outdoor market in Provence, France.

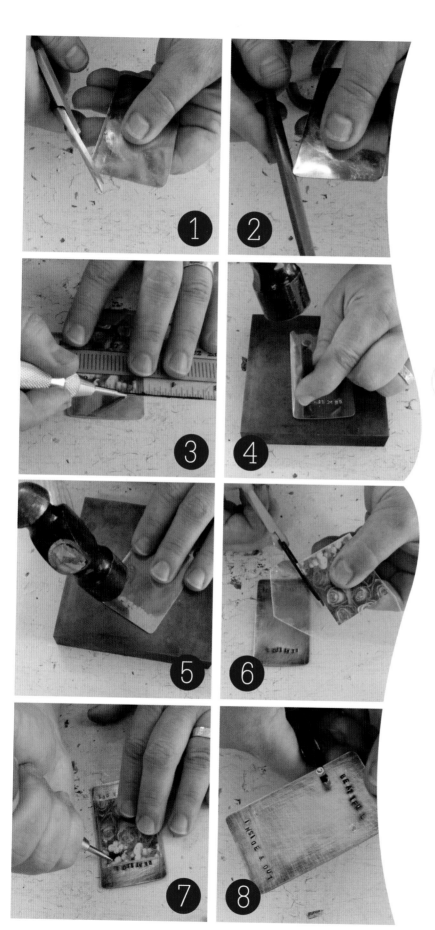

Tools

shears or jeweler's saw

file

ruler

metal letter stamp set

metal pattern stamp

dead-blow hammer

steel bench block

center punch

hole punch, 1/16" (2mm) or drill

ball-peen hammer

wire cutters

torch

round-nose pliers

Materials

20-gauge metal sheet, bronze

18-gauge wire, bronze

pearls

rhinestone rondelles

1/8" (3mm) short eyelets

1/16" (2mm) short eyelet

long nut and screw

image

mica

brass-casting charm

liver of sulphur

steel wool

1. Cut a piece of bronze sheet to 1¾" x 3" (4cm x 8cm). Snip the corners.

2. File the corners to make them rounded and file all edges to smooth.

3. Cut down an image to fit the metal, making it small enough so you can stamp words at the top and/or bottom of the metal. Holding the image in place, use a ruler to score a line on the metal at the top and the bottom of the image to mark where it will go.

4. Stamp out your words along the open spaces in the metal. Here I am placing letters for the phrase, "Beautiful inside & out."

5. When you're done stamping, turn the piece over and tap the stamped areas a bit with the hammer to flatten the piece back out. Note: Don't hammer too hard or you will completely flatten the letterforms.

6. Patina the metal and polish with steel wool. Cut a piece of mica slightly larger than your image. Note: You can also rip one or more sides of the mica to give a more rustic look if you like.

7. Mark for eyelet holes where you want to attach the image and mica to the metal. Here I am using a center punch to mark three holes.

8. Punch 1/16" (2mm) holes at the marks using a hole punch or drill.

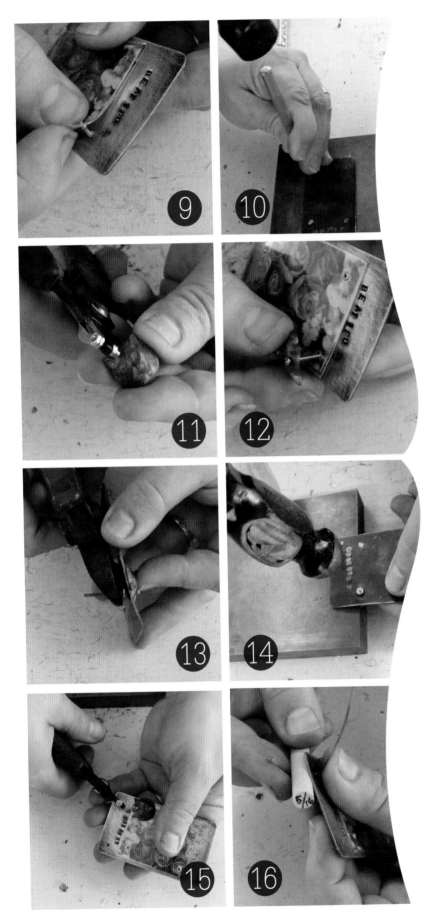

9. Insert the first eyelet from the front to the back through all three pieces.

10. Insert a second eyelet and carefully turn over the piece onto your steel block. Set the two eyelets with a hammer and eyelet setter. (Use the ball end of a ball-peen hammer to finish the eyelets.)

11. For the remaining hole, first punch or drill a hole in your charm.

12. Insert a long screw through the charm and the metal piece from the front to the back.

13. Tighten a nut onto the back. Cut the excess length of the bolt off using snips or wire cutters.

14. With the charm just off the block (so it doesn't get flattened), splay the end of the bolt a bit with the ball end of the ball-peen hammer to set the rivet.

15. Punch a hole in the top corners of the piece to hang the chain. Set the pendant aside.

16. Cut two 6" (15cm) pieces of wire and patina with heat. Draw a bead on one end of each to create two long headpins. Thread the first headpin through the pendant from the back to the front, leaving about 1" (3cm) from the ball end. Wrap the remaining length of wire around a ⁵⁄₁₆" or so (8mm or so) dowel to create the first loop.

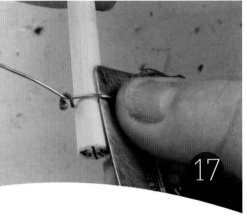  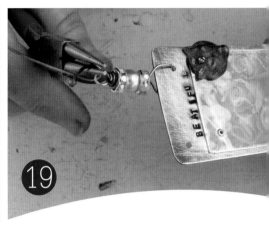

17. Overlap the wire and twist the ball end around the remaining length of the wire to close the loop.

18. Thread a rondelle spacer, a pearl and a second rondelle on the wire. Using round-nose pliers, make a loop above the beads.

19. Wrap the remaining wire in an organic fashion.

20. Cut twelve 4" (10cm) pieces of 18-gauge bronze wire. Make a metal fiber out of eleven of the pieces (draw a bead on both ends), and draw a bead on just one end of the last piece. Take one metal fiber and thread it through one of the beaded links attached to the pendant. Using round-nose pliers, make a loop at one end.

21. Wrap and cinch the ball end around the wire once to close the loop. Make a loop at the other end. Thread on a second metal fiber and start a loop in the same way. Continue with three more fibers. Repeat for the other side of the necklace chain. Create a hook clasp by making a loop end out of the last metal fiber and attach it to one end of the chain. With the remaining head pin, create a shepherd's hook and attach it to the other end of the chain to finish.

 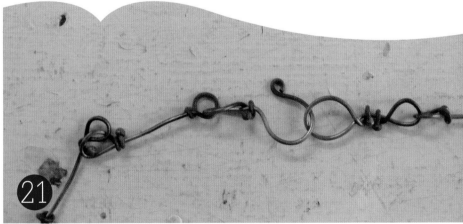

etched owl pendant

Micro bolts are a wonderful finding to add dimension and height to your work. This pendant goes from flat to fabulous with the subtle addition of four dapped and domed discs and micro bolt attachments for eyes. With the plethora of artsy rubber stamps available, etching is another way to incorporate mixed-media designs and textures onto plain sheet metal.

Tools

shears or jeweler's saw

file

metal letter stamp set

dead-blow hammer

ball-peen hammer

steel bench block

center punch

hole punch, 1/16" (2mm) or drill

permanent marker

flat-nose pliers

dapping set

wire cutters

torch

annealing pan

small mandrel or wooden dowel

round-nose pliers

needle-nose pliers

Materials

22-gauge metal sheet, brass

14-gauge wire, copper

20-gauge wire, bronze

24-gauge metal sheet, copper, etched with an owl image (see page 22 for more on etching)

24-gauge metal sheet, nickel

micro bolts, nuts and washers

Jax Brown patina

steel wool

1. Trim the etched owl piece to about 1" x 1½" (3cm x 4cm). Cut a piece of 24-gauge nickel to 2" x 1½" (5cm x 4cm). File the corners and edges if they are sharp. Set the etched piece onto the nickel and score a line where your wording will go.

2. To make centering your word easier, start by stamping the middle letter first, then working out from the center in both directions.

3. To deckle the edges of the nickel, use the ball end of a ball-peen hammer and tap lightly all around.

4. Patina the nickel piece and polish with steel wool. Center punch the eyes of the owl.

5. Punch holes at the marks. Place the owl piece onto the nickel and use it as a guide to mark for holes with a permanent marker.

6. Punch or drill holes out of the nickel.

7. Cut two 5/16" (8mm) discs from the brass sheet and two 1/4" (6mm) discs from the nickel sheet.

8. Use a dapping block to create tiny cups from the discs.

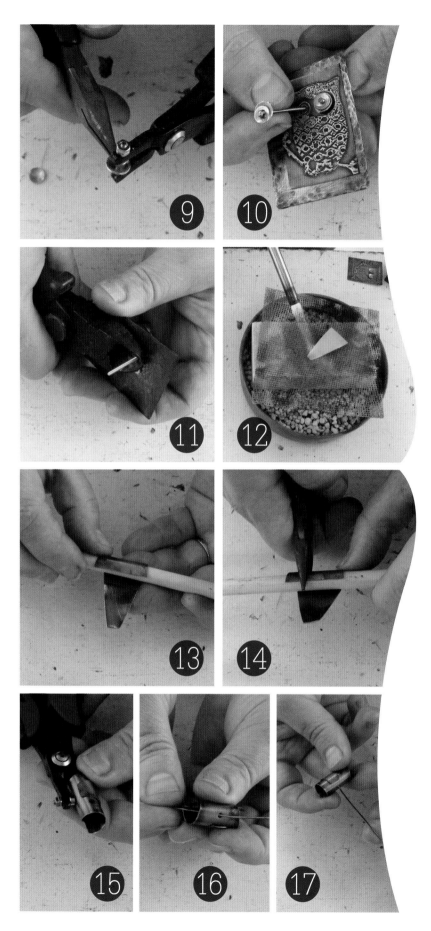

9. Punch holes in the centers of all four cups. Use pliers to gently remove the cups from the hole punch if necessary.

10. Thread micro bolts and washers through the small cups, the larger cups, the owl piece and then the nickel, and thread nuts on the back to secure.

11. Trim the excess bolts from the back using wire cutters.

12. Punch a hole at the top of the nickel piece. To make a bail, start by cutting a long triangular piece of 24-gauge copper sheet that is 2" (5cm) long and 1" (3cm) at the wide end. Anneal the copper piece using a torch.

13. Apply patina to the piece and polish. Hold a 5/16" (8mm) dowel at the wide end of the copper and start to wrap it.

14. Use pliers to help you firmly form the copper around the curve of the dowel.

15. Wrap the entire piece around the dowel then remove from the dowel. Punch or drill a hole in the center of the roll.

16. Cut a 5" (13cm) length of 20-gauge wire and draw a bead on one end. Thread the other end through the hole in the bail, from the inside to the outside.

17. Pull the wire through so that the bead on the wire stops at the inside of the bail.

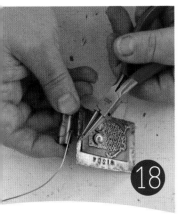   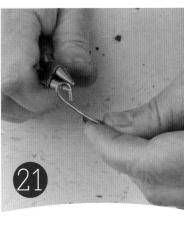

18. Thread the nickel onto the wire from the back of the piece to the front, and using round-nose pliers, make a loop close to the hole. Wrap the remainder of the wire in an organic fashion around the center of the wire.

19. The pendant is now complete.

20. To begin a neck wire to hold the pendant, first lightly work harden with a hammer on a steel block a 20"–24" (51cm–61cm) length of 14-gauge wire that you've formed into a U shape.

21. Thread the bail of the pendant onto the wire. Make simple loops on each end of the wire using round-nose pliers.

22. Cut a 4" (10cm) piece of 14-gauge wire. Using round-nose pliers, bend the wire in half.

23. Crimp the fold with flat-nose pliers. (Annealing the wire first makes it much easier to fold.) Work harden the folded wire using a hammer.

24. Create a hook at the folded end of the wire, using round-nose pliers.

25. At the other end, use the round-nose pliers to create a loop for attaching the hook to the neck wire.

26. Create three jump rings with additional copper wire. (See page 32.) Attach one jump ring to each end of the neck wire. Thread the hook onto one jump ring and the other jump ring will serve to catch the hook.

  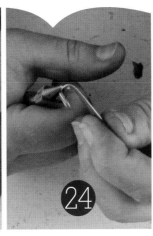 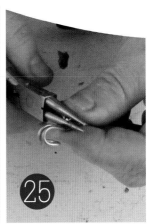 

tussy mussy cone necklace

Learning to form cones is a handy skill in metalsmithing because they can be used as end caps for leather cording, metal embellishments for tassels or even as focal pendants. In Victorian times when people weren't in the habit of bathing as frequently as today, women and men would carry small flower bouquets, called tussy mussies, to dip their noses into as a fragrant accessory to pungent smells. You can still find petite decorative metal cones from the era, which is what inspired this pendant.

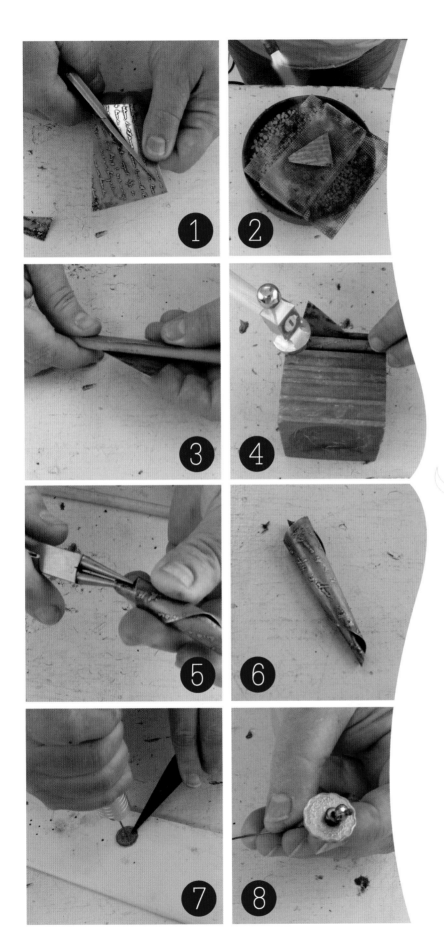

1. Cut an etched piece of 24-gauge brass into a triangle and snip off one end.

2. Anneal the piece.

3. Quench, pickle, patina and polish the triangle. Begin forming the triangle around a small mandrel to create a cone shape.

4. Using a forming block and a hammer helps to better start the shape.

5. Use round-nose pliers to tighten one end of the cone a bit to refine the shape.

6. The finished cone should be slightly more open at one end and more at a point on the other.

7. Center-punch the centers of two coins. Drill holes in the centers of the coins.

8. Thread a crystal, a spacer bead and one coin on a 22-gauge head pin.

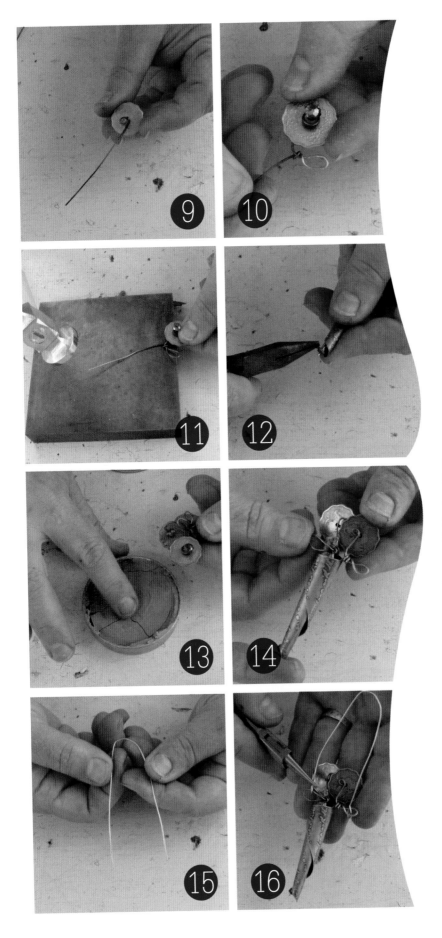

9. Using round-nose pliers, create a tiny loop at the back of the coin and crimp the loop.

10. Repeat for the other coin. At about ½" (13mm) from the coin, use flat-nose pliers to free-form a leaf shape.

11. Wrap the wire around the base of the loop a couple of times and the remaining wire will serve as the stem. Repeat for the other flower. Work harden the stems a bit using a hammer on a steel block.

12. Thread the stems through the cone from the inside out. Wrap one stem tightly around the other stem and crimp.

13. Apply gilder's paste to the coins for color.

14. Shape the leaves so they point out on each side of the cone.

15. Cut a 6" (15cm) length of 20-gauge wire and flatten a bit with a hammer. Form the wire into a U shape.

16. Using round-nose pliers, make a small loop on each end of the wire and connect the leaves to the loops. Crimp the ends closed.

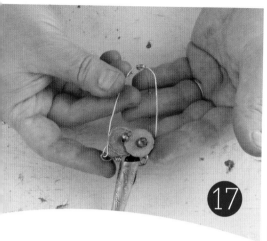
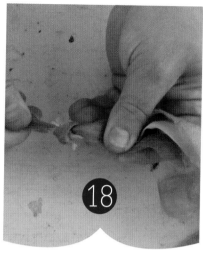
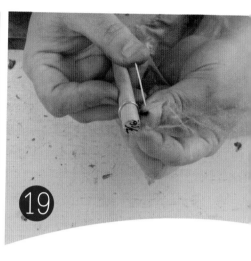

17. Create a 3" (8cm) metal fiber and wrap it around the top of the trapeze.

18. Cut or tear three 16" (41cm) pieces of sheer ribbon and knot them together in the center.

19. Cut two 6" (15cm) pieces of wire. Wrap one wire tightly around the ends of one half of the ribbon, and using a dowel, create a large loop in the wire.

20. Wrap the wire around the base of the loop and crimp.

21. Take the other wire and draw a bead on one end. Wrap the other end around the other half of the ribbon at the ends, and instead of a loop, create a hook using the dowel.

22. Work harden both halves of the clasp. Wrap a couple more metal fibers at the midpoints down each half of the ribbon length.

23. Thread a jump ring through the knot and thread on the pendant to finish.

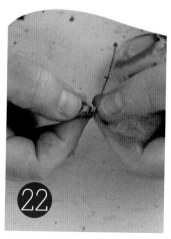

wire-stitched pendant

Now that you're gaining confidence in your metalworking skills, here's a project to put what you've learned into action. This necklace, with each component made by hand, is sure to become a signature piece that you're proud to wear. So many techniques are packed into this one project that it might seem overwhelming at first. This is where the important skill of learning how to look at all the components of a piece of jewelry and break them down becomes useful.

Tools

shears

file

disc cutter

drill and 1/16"
(2mm) bit

dapping set

dead-blow
hammer

ball-peen
hammer

wire cutters

steel bench block

texturizing
hammers

torch with MAPP
gas

annealing pan

flat-nose pliers

center punch

eyelet setter

riveting hammer

round-nose pliers

Materials

etched 22-gauge
metal sheet,
copper

etched 22-gauge
metal sheet,
brass

14-gauge wire,
bronze

22-gauge wire,
bronze

24-gauge wire,
colored

old skeleton keys

large decorative
beads

pave crystal
beads

clear crystal
beads

1/16" (2mm) short
eyelets

jump rings

silk ribbon

nickel pickle

Jax Brown patina

steel wool

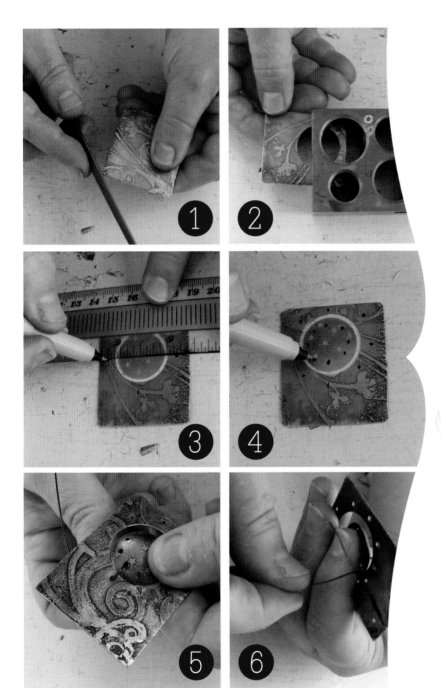

1. Cut a piece of etched copper to 1½" x 2" (4cm x 5cm) and file the corners to soften.

2. At about ¼" (6mm) from the center of one short end, punch a 1" (3cm) circle using a disc cutter.

3. Cut a ⅞" (2mm) circle from a piece of etched brass. Place the circle in the circular window of the copper piece. Mark for holes about ⅛" (3mm) from the edges. First find the vertical and horizontal center.

4. Now eyeball four more holes centered between the first four holes.

5. Drill a hole at each of the marks on each piece. Dap the circle a bit. You are now ready to sew the two together with wire. Cut a 36" (91cm) piece of 24-gauge colored wire and start threading it through the holes where they line up.

6. Twist the wire in back to secure it so you can sew more easily.

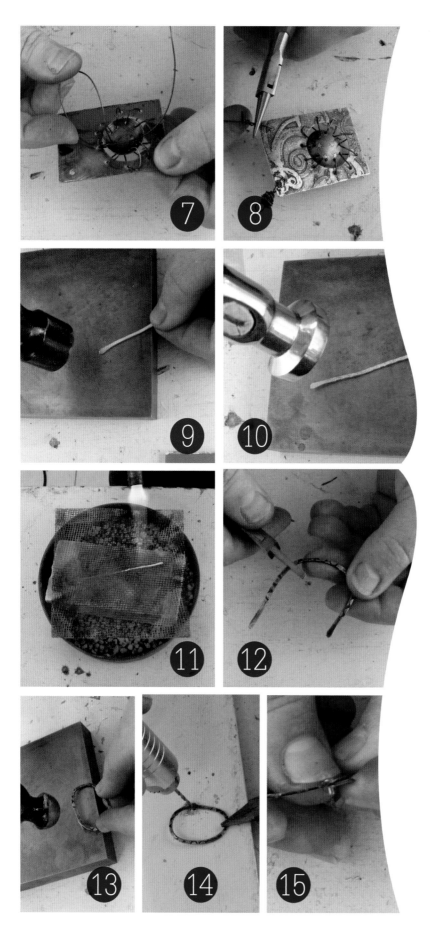

7. Whip stitch around the perimeter of the circle.

8. Drill a hole in each top corner. Cut two 12" (30cm) lengths of the same color wire. Create a loop on one end and thread it onto one corner of the metal piece. Wrap the tail around the wire, create a second loop with the remaining length and wrap that tail around the center. Repeat for the other hole and piece of wire.

9. Cut nine 4" (10cm) pieces of 14-gauge bronze wire. Forge the wires flat and paddle the ends. They should end up being wide enough to accommodate 1/16" (2mm) holes.

10. Use a "circles" texture hammer to give five pieces some texture.

11. Anneal these five pieces of flattened wire.

12. Quench and pickle the pieces, patina in Jax and polish. Using your hands and flat-nose pliers, form the pieces into flat links. Keep the metal flat as you work.

13. Work the shape until the ends overlap about 1/2" (13mm) and work harden where they overlap.

14. Center-punch and then drill a hole through both layers of the link.

15. Insert an eyelet through the hole.

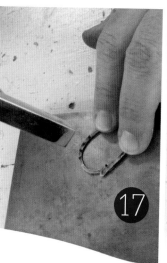
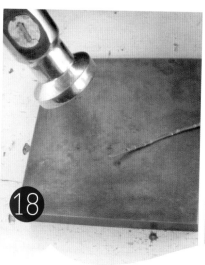

16. Turn the link and eyelet over so you can set it. Using a hammer and an eyelet setter, set the eyelet.

17. Finish it off with a riveting hammer.

18. For a bar link, forge a new piece of wire to flatten. You don't need to paddle the ends this time. Apply "lines" texture with a texturing hammer.

19. Anneal the textured bar.

20. Quench, pickle, patina and polish. Repeat steps 10–19 to complete four more circular links and three more bars. To begin assembling, begin a simple loop on one end of one bar with round-nose pliers and then insert a link into it. Cinch it closed with flat-nose pliers.

21. On the other end of the bar, repeat to attach another link.

22. Repeat with two more bars to connect a total of four links. Take the last bar and begin loops on each end. Bend the bar slightly into a flat U shape.

23. Set the fifth link aside. Using a spring-loaded center punch, mark for a hole at the bottom of the key. Drill a hole through the key. Repeat for the smaller key, putting the hole in the center of the key.

24. Draw a bead on a 5" (13m) length of 22-gauge wire, and on the bead end, make a small wrapped loop. Thread on a large decorative bead and then thread the wire through the hole at the end of the larger key.

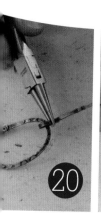

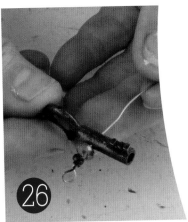

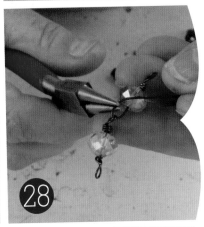

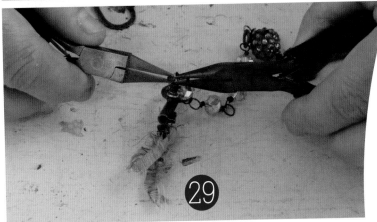

25. Create a second wrapped loop to close.

26. Repeat step 24 with a second wire, making a loop on the bead end, threading it through a bead, then through the hole in the smaller key.

27. Thread on additional beads and tie on a scrap of ribbon if you like. Then make a second wrapped loop to finish. Set the two key elements aside. Cut four 4" (10cm) pieces of colored wire. Using round-nose pliers, create a wrapped loop on one end. Thread on a crystal bead and then create a second wrapped loop and either trim the excess wire or wrap it until it runs out.

28. Begin a new link with one wrapped loop, thread on a bead, then thread the wire through one loop of the first link before finishing the wrapped loop.

29. Repeat for the other two links, creating a small chain of four crystals. Lay out all of the components in the order you would like them joined in the necklace. Connect each of the elements with jump rings. Keep in mind that one key can act as a toggle to close the necklace into one of the hammered links.

watch & learn

MICA BEZEL
Use the QR code here to see a video of Jen showing you how to make this project.

www.createmixedmedia.com/
makingmetaljewelry

dapped circles necklace

After making so many varied metal jewelry designs, you're sure to have a lot of interesting scraps on your workbench. With the cost of metal these days, the desire to get extra mileage from your supplies can also help you think outside the box when it comes to design. My starting point for this necklace was simply putting my scraps through my trusty disc cutter and stacking them up.

1. Punch out discs in a variety of sizes from a variety of different metals. You'll need approximately fifteen discs.

2. Using a permanent maker, draw a free-form crescent shape on a piece of metal sheet. (You won't see much of this when the necklace is finished, so it doesn't matter too much what it looks like.)

3. Cut out the shape using either shears or a jeweler's saw and file the edges. Deckle the edge with a ball-peen hammer.

4. Apply various textures to the circles, then dome all of them using a dapping block and polish.

5. Apply patina to all of the domed circles and polish with steel wool. Also add some color with gilder's paste. Punch or drill a hole in the center of each. (Smaller discs can usually be hand-punched; larger ones may need to be drilled.)

6. Begin nesting smaller discs into larger discs and laying out your composition on the crescent base, mixing the metals for contrast. Mark where holes on the base will go using the drilled holes in the discs as a guide.

7. Punch or drill the holes in the base.

8. Cut two 2" (5cm) pieces of 12-gauge wire and draw a bead on one end of each. Flatten the wire and the bead with a hammer. Flatten the non-bead end into a paddle as well.

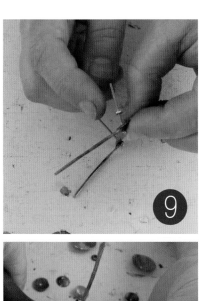

Tip

To keep all the nuts firmly into place, you may want to mix up a small amount of a jeweler's grade resin and apply a tiny dot to the tops of the nut and screw on the back of the crescent back plate. The resin is stronger than glue when cured and all those little discs are sure to stay in place forever.

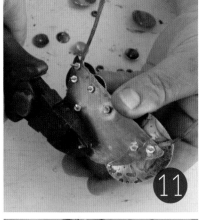

9. Drill a hole in each end of each wire. Attach the bead ends of the drilled wires to the base using micro bolts and nuts.

10. Trim the excess length of the bolt. Attach the discs to the base using micro bolts and nuts. Thread the bolts through from the front to the back, securing the nuts on the back. To create a variety of depths, stack some of the discs on top of spacer beads before threading the bolt through the base.

11. Tighten the nuts with flat-nose pliers, then trim the excess lengths from the bolts using flush cutters.

12. File the ends of the bolts so they will not feel rough against the skin when wearing the necklace. Cut three pieces of contrasting ribbon to 18" (46cm). Tie them together with a knot at one end, and tie a knot with a loop at the other end.

13. Cut the entire length in half. Cut two pieces of 20-gauge wire to 12" (30cm) and draw a bead on one end. Thread one wire through the hole in one of the hanging wires on the metal piece. Wrap the wire tightly around the cut ends of the ribbon, binding then together.

14. Thread the other wire through a spacer bead, then two discs, then through the knot end of the ribbon.

15. Check to see that the discs fit through the loop end of the ribbon.

16. Wrap the remaining wire around the ribbon. Wrap a final metal fiber around the base of the loop end of the ribbon.

watch & learn

HAMMERED CRESCENT VARIATION

Sometimes an unadorned piece of metal is as pretty as one covered in assorted textures and colors. For this variation, I refrained from covering the shape with domed discs. Instead, I deckled and formed the edges for a more minimal design.

house bezel pendant

The house is a shape I'm naturally drawn to, as my home is my haven. I'm so thankful for my home as it gives me shelter, provides a safe nest for my family and is where I do my creative work. Learning to make and solder your own bezels is an important technique in your metalsmithing toolbox, and the simple house shape is a wonderful project to practice your jeweler's saw skills.

1. Using a jeweler's saw, saw out the shape of a house from the sterling silver sheet.

2. Mark for the first side of your bezel wire using a permanent marker. Fold at the mark and continue around until you have a square bezel in the shape of the sawed metal house back piece. Cut the excess wire.

3. Ensure your bezel wire is resting flat on the metal back plate. Using a toothpick or piece of wire, apply eight dots of paste solder to the metal back piece where the bezel wire will be sitting against it.

4. Use the butane torch to solder the bezel wire to the house shape, being careful to keep the flame moving so as to not burn up the bezel wire.

5. Quench the piece and pickle. Add some texture to the top of the house using one or more metal stamps or a chisel and a hammer.

6. Punch a hole at the top.

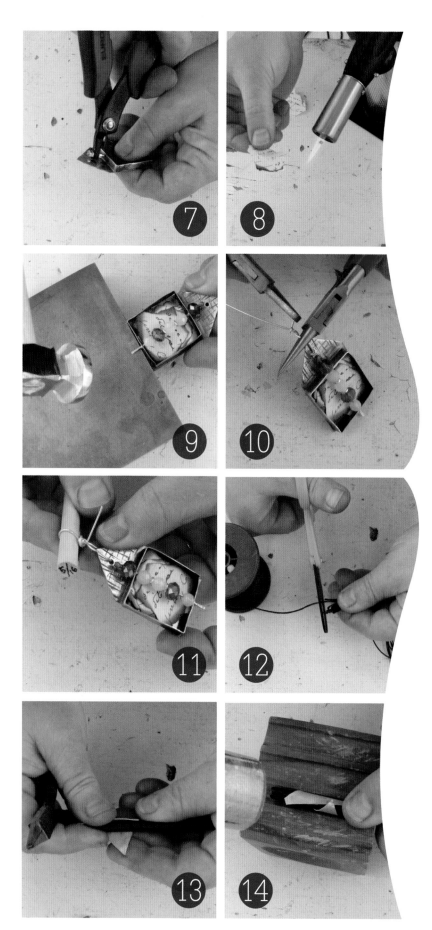

7. Patina in liver of sulfur and polish with steel wool. Punch a hole at the center top and bottom ends of the bezel.

8. Tear out three small squares of book text. Using a small torch or a candle, burn the edges of the paper stack. To do this safely, catch the edge of the paper on fire, and then quickly blow out the flame. Repeat until you have burned the entire perimeter.

9. Set the burnt paper in the bezel. Cut a 2" (5cm) piece of 18-gauge sterling wire and draw a bead on one end. Thread the wire though the top hole of the bezel and then through a series of beads and then out through the bottom hole. Paddle the end of the wire.

10. Cut a 4" (10cm) length of 20-gauge sterling silver wire. Thread the house onto the wire. Create one loop with round-nose pliers and wrap the tail around the wire.

11. Create a larger loop around a ⁵⁄₁₆" (8mm) dowel with the remaining wire and twist that tail around the center. When you're finished, the larger loop should be perpendicular to the loop on the house.

12. Cut eleven 16" (41cm) lengths of 1mm leather cord.

13. Using shears, cut two triangles from 24-gauge sterling silver sheet. Snip off the end of the long point of each. Anneal the triangles and pickle. Begin forming the triangles around a small dowel or dapping die.

14. To refine the cone shape, work with a hammer and the mandrel in a forming block.

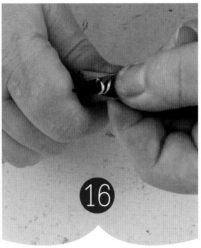

15. Continue to curl and shape the piece, now using round-nose pliers.

16. Add some texture to the cones with a ball-peen hammer, working on the round-nose pliers. Patina in liver of sulfur, and polish with steel wool. Cut two 3" (8cm) pieces of 18-gauge sterling wire. Make a small hook on one end of one wire. Insert the strands of leather into the hook and crimp the wire tightly, and then wrap it around the bundle a couple of times.

17. Bend the tail of the wire up (in a continuing line with the cord) and thread it on one cone.

18. Draw a bead on the end of the wire. Form the wire around a dowel to make a hook, then work harden it with a hammer on a steel block.

19. Cut a length of about 18" (sscm) of waxed linen. Wrap it tightly around a ¾" (19mm) wide section in the center of the cording. Tie a knot to secure.

20. Thread the pendant onto the cording. With a second 3" (8cm) piece of wire, wrap the other end of the cording, like you did in step 16. Thread on the other cone and draw a bead on that wire as well. Shape the wire around a ⁵⁄₁₆" (8mm) dowel to make a large loop. Wrap the tail around the base of the loop. Work harden the loop and you're done!

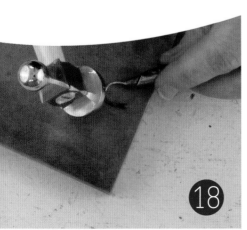

parting thoughts on art and going with the flow

When flipping through the projects in this book, a couple of concepts should be immediately clear. My artistic style is directly tied to the words I crafted for my artist statement: "Jen Cushman is drawn to the imperfect, the funky, the quirky, the artsy and the authentic—be it people or objects or art."

As my style has developed and my voice emerged, I've decided to call my work "organic." One of my dear friends calls it "messy but cool," which makes me chuckle. Fellow artist-friends of mine have used these adjectives: colorful, bohemian chic, textural and unconventional. Whatever it is or isn't doesn't really matter. What does matter to me is that it's imperfect.

I've struggled throughout my life with perfectionist tendencies, which I now know stem from this feeling I had as a young girl that I wasn't good enough. Good enough for what, I still can't tell you. I had an underlying feeling that I should be prettier, smarter, more talented. In high school and college, I learned to overcompensate for this by pushing myself hard in my chosen career of journalism. It also caused me to become a perfectionist in the things I did well. I continued in that vein throughout my twenties, only to find my life shift after having my son at thirty-one.

After I left my newspaper career to stay home with our son, I rediscovered my creative self, the person deep inside who simply loves to make stuff. As I learned new mixed-media techniques, my perfectionist tendency reared its ugly head. All those feelings of not being good enough swelled inside of me as I compared my art to others'. Through teaching, I've learned that many of us share the same insecurity. What I found in my life was that my need to make things perfect actually blocked my creative flow. It was almost as if self-doubt applied a tourniquet to my brain, cutting off my circulation so my hands simply could not produce what my heart desired.

I kept my passion for art quiet for a long time as I continued my writing career. I spent many hours studying the photos in my favorite craft books and magazine articles, desiring my work to look as beautiful as the featured artist's jewelry did in print. What I learned by staying focused on my dream and working out the kinks in the privacy of my sacred studio space is that the pressure I was placing on myself was truly—and there is no other word for it—nonsensical.

Years later, as I've settled into my authenticity, I can easily and publicly declare that, for me,

perfectionism is overrated. I find stunning beauty now in asymmetry, raw edges, rust and chipped paint, vintage fibers, cracked and broken objects, architectural salvage and works of art where a deeper, more intimate story is shared. What interests me now in my own work, as well as others' works I'm drawn to for inspiration, is seeing the hand of the artist, from the whole of the piece to the smallest of detail.

After trying your hand at several (or all) of the projects in this book, I hope you, too, can let your artistic voice sing in its full range of possibilities. While your journey may be different from mine, what draws us together with this book is our mutual desire for both knowledge and beauty.

resources

Susan Lenart Kazmer Art Mechanique
WWW.ICERESIN.COM

ICE Resin®, Bronze sheet metal, copper sheet metal, bronze wire, silver wire, bronze garter clips, bronze number nail head rivets, micro nuts and screws, ribbons and fibers, eyelets, heishi spacer beads.

Lonnie's Inc. Jewelry Supply
WWW.LONNIESINC.COM

Sterling silver sheet metal, nickel sheet metal, sterling silver wire, sterling silver bezel wire, Jax patinas, liver of sulfur, leather cording, Swarovski crystal beads, pearls.

Michele Goldstein Handmade Glass Beads
WWW.MICHELEGOLDSTEIN.COM

Baroque Art Gilder's Paste
WWW.GILDERSPASTE.COM

Jewelry Tools
WWW.JEWELRYTOOLS.COM

Disc cutter, dapping block, doming blocks and mandrels, forming block, texturizing hammers, chasing hammer, jeweler's files, bench pin, jeweler's saw, heavy-duty flush cutters, pliers, steel bench block, center punch, annealing pan and pumice stones, shears, butane torch.

index

acknowledgments

I'm living the life of my dreams. This is largely due to a handful of people who love me unconditionally and support my every endeavor. Abundant gratitude to: my soul mate, Greg, for being the love in my heart, the wind in my sails and my rock in every storm; my children, Ty and Izabella, for making me whole; my mother, Marg Cushman, for her love and my father, Bud Cushman, for telling me to "get on the stick" and write my Great American Novel. (Not there yet, Pops, but I'm heading in the right direction.) Additional gratitude to: my sister, Patti Stanley, for her encouragement; my mother-in-law, Kay, for taking care of my daughter while I work; and my dear friend Carol LaValley for being the Ethel to my Lucy. Last, but never least, to my business partner and jewelry mentor, Susan Lenart Kazmer, for changing my life.

I'd like to thank my editor, Tonia (Davenport) Jenny, for believing in me and being a sounding board for my ideas. I'm grateful to have been able to call her my friend long before I ever called her my editor. Also thanks to Kelly O'Dell for her beautiful design skills, and the rest of the folks behind the scenes at North Light Books who do their part to make artists' dreams of authoring books a reality.

EDITOR: TONIA JENNY
DESIGNER: KELLY O'DELL
PHOTOGRAPHER: JEN CUSHMAN
PHOTOGRAPHER: CAROL LAVALLEY
PRODUCTION COORDINATOR: GREG NOCK

Distributed in Canada by Fraser Direct
100 Armstrong Avenue
Georgetown, ON, Canada L7G 5S4
Tel: (905) 877-4411

Distributed in the U.K. and Europe by F&W Media International
Brunel House, Newton Abbot, Devon, TQ12 4PU, England
Tel: (+44) 1626 323200, Fax: (+44) 1626 323319
E-mail: enquiries@fwmedia.com

Distributed in Australia by Capricorn Link
P.O. Box 704, S. Windsor, NSW 2756 Australia
Tel: (02) 4577-3555

www.fwmedia.com

about jen cushman

Jen Cushman is a natural storyteller who found mixed-media art twelve years ago and never looked back. She is drawn to the imperfect, the funky, the quirky, the artsy and the authentic—be it people or objects or art. Jen began making metal jewelry in 2008 and continues to create collages and assemblages in addition to her metalwork. An enthusiastic and supportive instructor, she encourages others to explore their authentic, creative process to create personal work infused with imagery and storytelling.

Jen is the author of *Explore, Create, Resinate: Mixed Media Techniques Using ICE Resin®*, which won a bronze medal in the 2011 IPPY (Independent Book Publishers) national book awards in the Crafts/Hobby category. Her art has been published in *Belle Armoire Jewelry; Jewelry Affaire; Cloth, Paper, Scissors; Somerset Studio; Somerset Life; Create With Me; Mingle; WireWork* and others. Jen is also the Director of Education and Marketing for Susan Lenart Kazmer ICE Resin.

You can visit her website at www.jencushman.com or follow her blog at www.jencushman.wordpress.com. "Like" her "JenCushmanArtist" business page on Facebook or follow her on Twitter.

www.createmixedmedia.com/
makingmetaljewelry

create mixed media

Inspire your creativity EVEN FURTHER WITH THESE NORTH LIGHT TITLES.

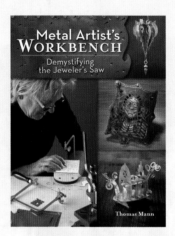

torch-fired enamel jewelry
by Barbara Lewis

Metal becomes your canvas as you learn the basics of enameling with a torch, then dive into 22 exquisite pieces, ranging from quirky "cattywampus" earrings to ethereal pendants to delicate multistrand necklaces. Find out how easy it is to create unique and colorful enamel pieces in this innovative, comprehensive guide to the world of torch-fired enameling.

metal artist's workbench
by Thomas Mann

Get to know the most diverse tools on your workbench— the jeweler's saw. With this comprehensive guide for creating jewelry and other sawn projects. Through exercises designed to get you "sawing in the zone," you'll be inspired to try your hand (and saw) at any of the 15 stepped-out projects.

tales of adornment
by Kristen Robinson

Incorporate resin into your jewelry designs with stunning results. You'll discover how to combine resin with mixed-media materials to create jewelry with depth and sophistication. Includes 18 step-by-step projects and 50+ jewelry-making techniques.

NORTH LIGHT BOOKS